轻 松 学 俗 语
Easy Way to Learn Chinese
Slang

申俊 马汉民 编

Compiled by
Shen Jun and Ma Hanmin

新 世 界 出 版 社
NEW WORLD PRESS

First Edition 1998
Idea Created by Jiang Hanzhong
Edited by Song He
Illustrations by Liu Yang
Book design by Zhu Anqing

ISBN 7-80005-373-3

Published by
NEW WORLD PRESS
24 Baiwanzhuang Road, Beijing, 100037, China

Distributed by
CHINA INTERNATIONAL BOOK TRADING CORPORATION
35 Chegongzhuang Xilu, Beijing, 100044, China
P.O. Box 399, Beijing, China

Printed in the People's Republic of China

前　　言

　　俗语,是中国民间文化艺术宝库中的一颗明珠。它通俗简炼,形象生动,既说明某种事理,又具有很强的艺术表现力。它主要来源于口语,是人民群众智慧和想象力的结晶。俗语,顾名思义,往往是一个民族社会习俗的反映,与其历史背景和文化因素密切相关。很多俗语的产生、发展及演变,都伴随着一个美丽的故事或传说。这些俗语连同它们的故事长久地在民间流传下来,活跃在人们的日常用语中,成了汉语语汇中不可缺少的重要组成部分。

　　本书编者精选了现代汉语中常用的 60 多条俗语,中英文相对照,以故事的形式,详尽地说明了它们的来历、涵义和用法。一些故事还配有生动形象的插图,以帮助读者理解和记忆。为方便外国读者阅读和理解,编者对俗语词条中的汉字加注了拼音,并对故事中涉及到的历史、文化名词给出了简明的注释。

　　对于那些正在学习汉语,或是对中国文化感兴趣的外国人来说,本书就象一幅中国民俗画的长卷,向他们展示着中国民间的文化和习俗,令他们在轻松的欣赏之余,领略中国文化的魅力,同时丰富其汉语语汇,提高其中文的语言表达能力。因而,本书可以作为外国人学习汉语的趣味性读物。

　　另外,本书的英文部分出自有经验的翻译之手,并经外国专家润色,准确、流畅、生动、优美。因此,本书也可作为中国人学习英语的辅助读物,能使读者在掌握一些俗语的英译法的同时,学到纯正、地道的英文,从而提高英语的口语和书面表达能力,以便更加自如地与外国朋友进行交流。

FOREWORD

Chinese slang sayings are gems in the treasure house of Chinese folk culture. They have come from the Chinese folk and have been playing an active role in people's daily lives. Being closely related to the historical and cultural background of China, they vividly reflect the customs of Chinese society. Most of them have been derived from a beautiful and intriguing tale and have spread far and wide with the tale itself.

This book includes about 60 different slang sayings, which are commonly used in modern Chinese language. With the story following each of the slang sayings and the illustrations accompanying some of them, the reader can gain a distinct idea about every slang saying and get to know how to use them in the correct way. To enhance comprehension of the readers whose mother tongue is not Chinese, the compilers have marked each Chinese character with *pinyin* and offered concise notes on the historical and cultural terms involved in the stories.

In addition to displaying a panorama of Chinese folk culture and social customs, this book also provides the foreign readers with a chance to get acquainted with the *living* Chinese language. By reading this book and trying to employ the slang sayings in everyday conversation, the foreign readers will find their Chinese friends amazed and impressed, and thus become more confident in the study of the Chinese language.

Furthermore, the English translation of this book has been proofread by Melinda Arnott, an Australian expert who is proficient in Chinese language, and thus it presents fluent and elegant English to readers. Therefore, it can help Chinese readers to improve their spoken and written English, enabling them to communicate with foreign friends more freely.

目 录
CONTENTS

吃　醋

chī　　cù

EATING VINEGAR

魏征是唐朝的开国元勋,因他劳苦功高,贞观年间(627-649)唐太宗封他为左光禄大夫、郑国公。他虽官居极品,可不像那些得志的小人,一旦荣华富贵,不是休妻另娶,就是讨三房四妾,他还是和妻子恩爱如初。

唐太宗知道此事后,一天早朝后把魏征单独留下,要赐他几名美女为妾。魏征百般推辞,唐太宗就是不依。两人正相持不下,突然听见有人高叫:"陛下,魏大哥不要,你就将美女赐与我吧!"唐太宗一见是程咬金,不由大怒,喝令他退下。程咬金越想越气,他匆匆赶到郑公府,将此事向魏夫人说了一遍。

魏夫人一怒之下,穿戴上凤冠霞帔,随程咬金闯上金殿,质问唐太宗为何拆散他们恩爱夫妻,并说:"陛下硬要郑公纳妾,臣妾不如死了好。"唐太宗说:"好,我成全你。"随即命内侍到后宫取他亲手配的毒酒。

程咬金见此,怕太宗真地毒死魏夫人,偷偷溜了出来。不一会儿,内侍端着一壶毒酒来到,正和程咬金撞了个满怀,把壶摔得粉碎。程咬金忙递过另一个酒壶,让他呈上去。魏夫人将一壶毒酒一饮而尽。

魏夫人只想着马上就要死了,谁料过了好半天,毒性也没发作,只觉得口中酸溜溜的不是味。程咬金大笑着说:"大嫂如此能吃醋,真是个醋缸。"

太宗大惊,忙问内侍,才知酒壶被程咬金换过了,不由微微一笑说:"只可惜了我那壶百花露。"

原来唐太宗并不是真想毒死魏夫人,只想和她开个玩笑,让内侍取来的是百花露,而程咬金信以为真,用一壶醋换下了百花露。

这就是"吃醋"的来历。本来,魏夫人吃醋是为了捍卫真挚的爱情,可是后来,"吃醋"的词义发生了变化,人们用它来形容恋爱中的男女的嫉妒心理。

During the Zhenguan Period of the Tang Dynasty (627-649), Wei Zheng was conferred by Emperor Tai Zong the titles of the Left Grand Councilor and Duke of the State of Zheng because of his dedication and valuable service in founding the Tang Dynasty. Indeed Wei Zheng was a man of great integrity and did not seek corrupt pleasure as many officials did. Wei Zheng refused to take any concubines or forsake his first wife, on the contrary, he remained faithful to his beloved wife. He also rejected the life of privilege, wealth and luxury, which many lesser men had greedily embraced after their rise in feudal hierarchy.

Emperor Tai Zong decided to test Wei Zheng's fidelity. One day, after attending court, he invited Wei Zheng to stay behind and offered him some beautiful maidens to be his concubines. Wei Zheng immediately declined the offer. The emperor pressed his offer but Wei Zheng stuck to his position. During their conversation a third voice was heard: "Please Your Majesty, will you give me the concubines, since elder brother Wei does not want them?" pleaded Cheng Yaojin, a boisterous general in the founding period. The Emperor was enraged by this insolence, and he curtly instructed Cheng to leave the court and to mind his own business.

Cheng was infuriated and rushed to the residence of the Duke of Zheng to tell Madam Wei Zheng of the imperial offer to her husband. Madam Wei Zheng put on her court dress and went to see the Emperor with Cheng Yaojin. She demanded the Emperor offer her a reason as to why he should want to break up her happy and loving marriage. Madam Wei declared that if the emperor forced Duke of Zheng to adopt concubines she would rather die. The Emperor responded with: "Very well then, you shall have your way" and he then asked his eunuch to bring in a bottle of poisonous wine which he had mixed himself for Madam Wei to drink. Cheng Yaojin feared that the Emperor would really poison her. He tried to divert Madam Wei's fate and purposefully bumped into the eunuch carrying the bottle of poisoned wine which broke into pieces. Cheng then replaced the broken bottle with a bottle of vinegar. The eunuch handed it to Madam Wei and she drank it in one gulp. She then waited to die but nothing happened, except for the strong acidic taste in her mouth. Cheng Yaojin then remarked that it was remarkable Madam Wei could drink so much vinegar. The Emperor was as confused as Madam Wei and asked the eunuch to explain what was going on. The Emperor smiled at the antics but remarked that it was a shame to have wasted the "poisonous" hundred flower juice he had personally prepared. Actually the Emperor did not really intend to poison Madam Wei, he was merely amused to see how far her love would go.

Cheng Yaojin's credulousness and replacement of the hundred flower juice with vinegar has become a story with meaning for many jealous lovers. Madam Wei's faithful love was so strong that she would even drink poison to defend it. But over the generations it has become a vulgar slang which means being jealous of a rival in love.

两　面　派

liǎng　miàn　pài

A TWO – FACED CHARACTER

元朝末年，元军和朱元璋（明朝的开国皇帝）领导的义军在黄河北面，展开了拉锯战。这可苦了这一带的老百姓，元军来了要欢迎，义军来了也要欢迎。贴在门上的红红绿绿的欢迎标语，来得勤，换得也快。

河南北部的怀庆府人生活节俭，舍不得花钱买纸写欢迎标语。他们想出了一个好办法，用一块薄薄的木板，一面写着"欢迎元军保境安民"，另一面却写"驱除鞑虏，恢复中华"。哪方面来了，就翻出欢迎哪方面的标语，既省钱，又方便。

有一次，常遇春率领义军打跑了元军，进驻怀庆府。一进城见家家门口五颜六色的木牌上，全是欢迎义军的标语，他很高兴。突然一阵狂风刮来，木牌被吹翻过来，常遇春一看木牌反面全是欢迎元军的标语，非常生气，下令凡门口挂两面牌的满门抄斩。

常遇春下令假装撤退，在大街上扔下元宝，一会儿再回来，元宝没有了，见人就杀。再扔元宝再撤退，有人拾走元宝，再抓去杀。就这样直杀得没人再敢拾元宝为止。这样怀庆府还能剩多少人呢？这就是明初由山西洪洞县往这里移民的一大原因。

现在我们说的"两面派"就是从怀庆府挂"两面牌"演变而来的。人们用它形容对斗争双方都敷衍的人。

In the line of dynasties the Ming succeeds the Yuan. At the end of the Yuan Dynasty (1271-1368), there was much fighting. The Yuan troops had waged a seesaw battle in the region north of the Yellow River against the forces of Zhu Yuanzhang, who later became the Emperor of the Ming Dynasty (1368-1644). It was a confusing time for the people of this region as they were expected to greet whichever army that occupied their township. Every time the occupying army entered they had to put up banners with welcoming slogans. In this period of uncertainty, the banners were used all too frequently.

The people in Huaiqing Prefecture in northern Henan Province led a frugal life and hated to write a welcome banner every time a new army entered. So they thought of a way to economize. Instead of using paper, they used a wooden board which they could recycle. On one side of the board, they wrote, "We welcome the Yuan army to protect the region and bring peace to the people." On the other side, they wrote, "Drive out the Tartars and restore the middle kingdom!" It could be turned over and back again at appropriate times. This was an economic and convenient way for the people to fulfill their patriotic duties.

Soon after, the insurrectionary army under the command of General Chang Yuchun defeated the Yuan court troops. The General and his soldiers entered the seat of Huaiqing Prefecture and were greeted with the colorful wooden boards to welcome them. Suddenly, there was a gust wind and the wooden boards were flipped over. The General saw the words welcoming the Yuan court troops written on the other side of the board. He was enraged and ordered punishment for the families that had written the words on both sides of the board.

Chang Yuchun then feigned that he was withdrawing from the town. He tricked the people by leaving shoe-shaped silver ingots on the streets. Those who took the ingots were then accused of theft when the General returned. He then proceeded to kill the "thieves". He played this trick again and again. The killing went on until no one dared to pick the silver ingots which were left abandoned on the street. As a result of this, the prefecture of Huaiqing was left with only a few inhabitants. That was why when the Ming Dynasty was formally established, many people migrated from Hongdong County in neighboring Shanxi Province to Huaiqing.

This story later gave rise to the expression "a two-faced character". It was once used to describe the dilemma of a man who has a foot in both camps, and now refers to a dual character currying favor with both sides.

花 架 子

huā   jià   zi

A SHOWY STRUCTURE

元朝时候,上海松江乌泥泾出了个纺织家黄道婆(1245-?)。她的纺织技术名扬天下。在她的带动下,乌泥泾一带,男女老少都织布,一派兴旺景象。

镇上有个李秀才,出身书香门第,认为操机弄梭是小人所为,不屑一顾。因此,他虽然生活穷困,却不学纺织,只希望有朝一日金榜题名。然而他几上考场,总是名落孙山,眼看家中断粮,经人介绍,才去浙江湖州织里当教师。织里是纺织之乡,村里人知道他是乌泥泾人,纷纷找他求教纺织新技术。

这一来难煞了李秀才,只得把黄道婆的经历胡吹了一通。他说黄道婆的新式织布机他看见过,可以画在纸上,叫木匠照样做了,让大家学着使用。村民们信以为真。

李秀才花了半天工夫,总算把新机画成了。村民们高高兴兴地请来高明的木工,制作了一架织布机。那木机果然式样新颖,设计别致,大家看了无不拍手叫好。可是,村里最灵巧的织妇也不会用它织布,李秀才却说织里的人手脚笨。就这样折腾了好几天,还是不能用。村民们只好把那架木机搁在那儿。

后来,黄道婆的纺织技术和新式织布机真正传到了织里,人们才知道李秀才根本不懂纺织工艺。他画的那架木机,式样很花哨,却不能使用,所以村里人把它叫做"花架子"。

从此,在浙江一带流传开了"花架子"一语,专门指那些中看不中用的工具和行为。

During the Yuan Dynasty, there lived a woman textile engineer in Wunijing, Songjiang County (now under the jurisdiction of greater Shanghai municipality). People called her Aunty Huangdao. With excellent technique, Aunty Huangdao personally helped to establish a thriving textile industry in Wunijing. Absolutely everyone took part — male, female, old or young — and consequently the town prospered.

In the same town, there was a young scholar by the name of Li. He had passed the feudal county examination and was waiting to sit for another examination to prepare for an official career in the feudal hierarchy. Li was a very poor man but came from a family of intelligentsia. He therefore thought it was below him to learn the textile trade. He took the provincial examination many times but failed. He soon ran out of food and had nothing to feed his hungry stomach. He was forced to work as a tutor in Zhili in the neighboring Zhejiang Province to make a living. Zhili produced silk and the townsfolk asked Li to teach them the advanced method of weaving from Wunijing, the famous textile center. This put Li on the spot as he was completely clueless about the techniques of the textile trade. Despite this, he spoke at length about the technique of Aunt Huangdao and even said that he could easily draw a copy of the weaving machine. Everybody believed what Li had told them was true.

Li spent half a day drawing his machine. The people saw the specimen on paper and asked a highly-skilled carpenter to make the machine. When the machine was finished, everybody believed it was the latest and most advanced model of weaving machine. However, no one in Zhili — no matter how clever, could operate the new machine. Li said that the people could only blame themselves for this and attribute it to their own stupidity. The people attempted for a few more days before finally giving it up. They left the machine alone and put it aside.

Subsequently Aunty Huangdao's textile technique spread to Zhili and the new weaving machine arrived in the county. The people there discovered that Li actually knew nothing about weaving techniques. The specimen he drew up was fancy and flashy but not functional. They called it "a showy structure" — something dazzling to the eye but has no practical value. The phrase can be used to describe an object as well as a person's behavior.

吹 牛 皮

chuī niú pí

BLOWING INTO THE COW HIDE

"吹牛皮"说的是黄河河套地区,人们用牛羊皮做成筏子。过河之前,用足力气往筏子里吹气,然后人坐在上面就可以渡河。吹牛皮筏子实在是件十分吃力的事情,因而当地流传着两句话,讽刺那些无所事事,好撒谎、说大话的人:"你有闲工夫还是去吹牛皮筏子吧!"和"好大的口气,简直可以吹胀一个牛皮筏子!"这两句话几经流传就形成了"吹牛皮"一语。

可是在江苏,渡河从来不用牛羊皮筏子,这"吹牛皮"一语又是从何而来的呢?

明末年间,吴县有个地主叫谢金余,他依仗自己的丈人在朝里做官,平日横行乡里,无恶不作。这年,他的丈人即将告老回乡,谢金余就想为他建造一个花园。谢金余看中了与他毗邻的徐寡妇家的三亩薄田。可是徐寡妇人虽穷,却有骨气,就是不卖这三亩耕田。为此谢金余怀恨在心。正当插秧灌水时节,谢金余断了徐家周围的水道,徐家只得用水车车水救秧;正当稻熟季节,谢金余又放出鸡鸭鹅来啄食徐家稻谷;到收割时,谢金余趁月黑风高,指使狗腿子把徐家的禾稻践踏得一片狼藉。第二天,徐寡妇一看便知是谢金余所为,于是找到谢家,拉了谢金余就去见官。这一年担任县令的是一个姓苏的赃官,人称"说不清"。徐寡妇说了缘由之后,县官就让谢金余申辩,谢金余竟然说禾稻全是老鼠糟蹋的。徐寡妇说:"一夜就把三亩禾稻全糟蹋光,有这样大的老鼠吗?"谢金余竟胡说道:"穷家的老鼠大得可以和牛相比呢。"虽然谢金余强词夺理,赃官总是偏袒他。徐寡妇的官司是输了,但穷人的嘴是封不住的:"老鼠竟然大得可以和牛相比,我们就叫他'鼠牛比'吧!"这段故事就传开去了。吴县人从此便把如此这般荒诞不堪的人和事称作"鼠牛比"了。

"鼠牛比"和"吹牛皮"不仅所指内容相近,而且在吴语中语音又相同,于是"鼠牛比"就渐渐变成"吹牛皮"了。

The Chinese expression "blowing into the cow hide" (*chui niu pi*) has two unusual stories behind it.

When crossing the river, the people of the Yellow River Bend would use cow or sheep hide to make a raft. To make the hide floatable required air to be blown into it, which was a very demanding task. The local people would ridicule those who boast and brag by saying, "If you have so much time to brag, you'd better spend the day more constructively by inflating the cow hide. How big you talk! You could blow up a cow hide with all of that air!" "Blowing into the cow hide" (*chui niu pi*) has thus become the expression for bragging. The equivalent expression in English is "being full of hot air".

The people of Jiangsu Province do not inflate cow hides but they also use this expression the same way. The story goes that a landlord by the name of Xie Jinyu lived in Wuxian County, Jiangsu Province, towards the end of the Ming Dynasty. He rode roughshod in the county, committed numerous atrocities and escaped punishment because of his father-in-law's influence as an official in the capital. His father-in-law was about to retire from the official hierarchy so Xie Jinyu wanted to build a garden for him. Xie wanted to use the three *mu* of land belonging to his neighbor, a widow by the name of Xu. Although the widow was poor, she was very proud and refused to sell the land to Xie Jinyu. The landlord was enraged and bitter about the widow. In revenge, he cut the water supply from her land during planting season. The widow had to use a waterwheel to water her land. When the rice was ready for harvest, Xie Jinyu let loose a flock of ducks and chickens to pick the rice seeds. Then during harvest time, he sent his underlings to trespass and tramp on her rice field. The widow found this out the following day and knew very well that this was the work of her troublesome neighbor. She took the landlord to the local official to file her complaint.

Su, the magistrate happened to be a corrupt official, nicknamed "one to whom none could make his case clear". Widow Xu told the magistrate of her complaint. Xie Jinyu, however, said that it was the rats that had eaten her crops. The widow refuted this, saying that there was no rat big enough to eat so many crops in one night. Xie Jinyu replied, "This rat must be as big as a cow." Alas, the widow lost her case. She told many people of her case, saying that it was impossible that a rat can be as big as a cow. The story spread far and wide. The people of Wuxian County began to call those who told tall tales "*shu niu bi* (comparing a rat with a cow)".

As "*shu niu bi*" and "*chui niu pi*" are not only same in meaning but also similar in pronunciation in the Jiangsu dialect, the former has gradually been replaced by the latter in people's everyday speech.

拍 马 屁

pāi   mǎ   pì

PAT THE BACK OF THE HORSE

明朝天启年间（1621-1628），太监魏忠贤有一套高超的驯马本领。当时，他还不十分得宠，于是就奏请皇上在西校场赛马，想利用自己骑马的本事来讨皇上欢心。正好皇帝闲得发慌，于是降旨，命京城武官参加赛马。

九月九日，重阳佳节，正是赛马的大好时光。成群结队的老百姓都到西校场来看热闹。天启皇帝身穿龙袍，端坐在辇车上，百官相随来到西校场。随着三声炮响，几百匹马像离了弦的箭，直往前蹿。马上的武官个个精神抖擞，高举马鞭向马背上拼命抽打，噼啪声响成一片。

魏忠贤待炮声响后，翻身上马，他手不挥鞭，只是在马屁股上轻轻拍了三下，就见坐骑四蹄腾空，快如闪电，往前追去，眨眼工夫就把别人的马匹远远地甩在后面，跑到终点。顿时全场沸腾，人人称奇。

天启皇帝问魏忠贤为何不用鞭子就能取胜，是哪里弄来的神马。魏忠贤答道："我的马并不是神马，我能遥遥领先，主要是识得马性。要马跑得快，千万不能打，只需在马屁股上轻轻拍三下。驾马妙法就是"拍马屁"。

天启皇帝听了笑道："你能知性畜灵性，顺其性而驾之，是个大材大器。自你进宫以来，所办之事，件件令我称心如意。从今以后，朝廷内外，事无大小，一律归你掌管。"魏忠贤听后三呼万岁。

魏忠贤能识马性，也能明白天启皇帝的心事，拍得皇帝称心如意。因此天启皇帝也越来越宠爱魏忠贤。从此魏忠贤掌管朝政，倒行逆施，显赫一时。老百姓都讲魏忠贤能到这步田地，就是拍马屁拍来的。从此，"拍马屁"这句俗语也就在民间流传开来了，人们用它形容谄媚奉承的行为。

Eunuch Wei Zhongxian, who lived in the reign of Emperor Tianqi of the Ming Dynasty, had a special skill in taming horses. He had not found favor with the emperor and was looking for an opportunity. He requested the monarch hold a horse race in the western drill ground in the capital, hoping to find favor with the Emperor by displaying his fine horsemanship. One day the Emperor wanted to while away his time so he finally gave the order to hold a horse racing event.

On the double 9th festival — 9th day of the 9th lunar month — the event was held. It was a relaxed occasion on account of the fine autumn weather. People turned out in the thousands to watch this exciting event. Emperor Tianqi arrived in a chariot, wearing a dragon robe, accompanied by hundreds of his officials. At the sound of three cannon shots hundreds of horses galloped forward. The officers put on a militant display by lashing the horses with whips to urge them to go faster and faster. The sound of whipping pierced the air.

Wei Zhongxian also galloped out at the sound of the cannon but did not use his whip. Instead he used a different technique of patting his horse on the back three times. Wei Zhongxian and his horse galloped ahead leaving all of the other horses behind. When he reached the finish line, the sound of hooray thundered from the crowd, who all marveled at his brilliance.

Emperor Xizong asked Wei Zhongxian why he did not use the whip and where did he acquire such a fine horse. Wei replied that his horse was just an ordinary one but that he knew the nature of horses and could easily ensure the horses' victory. He firmly believed that a good jockey should not whip the horse; the best way to ride a horse is to pat the back of the horse.

The emperor smiled at Wei Zhongxian's ingenuity and said, "Indeed, you do know the nature of horses and you know how to ride the horse in accordance with its nature. You are a wonderful man. You have done everything to my satisfaction since you entered the palace and from now on I shall entrust you with all major tasks in the court." Wei Zhongxian exclaimed "Long live the emperor" three times in exaltation and gratitude.

Wei Zhongxian certainly did know the nature of horses. He also knew what kind of man the emperor was. He flattered the emperor a great deal and the emperor began to favor Wei Zhongxian more and more. After Wei Zhongxian took over the control of court duties he sauntered around brimming over with self-satisfaction. People knew that Wei had found great favor with the emperor by patting the back of the horse. Later "Pat the back of the horse" became a colloquialism meaning to flatter somebody.

敲 竹 杠

qiāo zhú gàng

RAPPING BAMBOO POLES

清代道光年间，一些西方人将大量鸦片运到中国来，毒害中国人民。以林则徐（1785-1850）为首的禁烟派，竭力主张禁绝鸦片烟，最后得到了朝廷的支持。林则徐一面派军队把守各个港口、海关，一面派专职人员在内地各码头稽查走私活动。

有一天，一处泊船码头上来了个人，肩上扛着好几根捆在一起的毛竹杠，吃力地走上了船。上船后，他把竹杠子放下，自己坐在上面。这时候，有一个乡下老汉上船后，也朝毛竹杠上坐下去，漫不经心地吸着旱烟。

船还没开，只见一队巡查禁烟人员上了船，四处观察人们的行李。扛竹杠子的人见了，脸上露出惊慌的神色，恰好此时老汉又将刚吸完了烟的旱烟锅头在毛竹上敲了几下，扛毛竹的人更慌张了，立即从口袋里掏出一把钱来，悄悄塞给老汉。老汉倒被他弄得莫名其妙。那人硬把钱塞到老汉手里，才放心地坐在竹杠子上，直到巡查队上岸而去。

原来，这个人扛的毛竹杠子里面的竹节已全被打通，塞满了鸦片烟，准备走私赎卖出去。当老汉无意中当着巡查人员的面，用烟锅头敲竹杠的时候，那人只当老汉知道此事了，所以马上塞给他一大笔钱，求他不要声张出来。其实老汉一点也不知道毛竹杠内的秘密。后来，人们用"敲竹杠"来形容利用别人的弱点或借某种口实索取财物。

In the reign of Emperor Daoguang (1821-1851) during the Qing Dynasty, there was a flourishing opium trade controlled by Western merchants. Lin Zexu (1785-1850), the head of a group of Chinese court officials, vehemently opposed this notorious and illegal trade that was ruining many Chinese people. He won the support from the monarch to suppress trafficking. Lin sent soldiers to all ports to prevent opium from entering into China. The Chinese customs officials patrolled and searched all wharves in an effort to stop the trade and hunt down the traffickers.

On one occasion a man shouldering a bundle of bamboo poles boarded a boat. Then he put down the bamboo poles and sat on the top of the pile. An elderly country bumpkin also decided this would be a good place to sit and smoke his pipe.

A team of customs officers boarded the ship, scrutinizing the luggage and cargo on the boat. The bamboo pole carrier instantly showed signs of fear on his face. At that moment, the bumpkin finished with his smoking and rapped the ashes on the bamboo to clean his pipe. Seeing this, the man suddenly became very anxious. He took out some money from his pocket and surreptitiously handed it to the bumpkin. The bumpkin was still a little baffled, but the man insisted that he should accept the money. And when he did, the man seemed relieved and sat back on his bamboo poles, and when the officials left the boat he completely regained his composure.

Obviously, the bamboo was full of opium. The bumpkin was an unwitting receiver of bribe money. The trafficker thought that he had learned his secret and so gave him money to keep his mouth shut.

By and by, "rapping bamboo poles" came to symbolize extortion. That is the fleecing of money from someone who, being in a perilous position, has to pay money to cover themselves.

露 马 脚
lòu　　mǎ　　jiǎo

SHOW THE CLOVEN HOOVES

相传黄帝治世时，百兽驯服，虎不伤人、蛇不横道。黄帝出巡时，凤凰伴驾，六龙拉车，威武凶猛的狮子为他充当前卫，就连桀骜不驯的苍鹰也在黄帝的辇车左右飞来飞去，鼓动翅膀为黄帝扇凉。但是美中不足的是：主祥兆瑞的麒麟却一直不肯来归服。为这件事，黄帝一直不快乐。后来，这件事被马知道了，于是它找来一张麒麟皮，披在身上，把自己打扮成麒麟的样子，来见黄帝。黄帝见到这只麒麟后，喜动天颜，命人将其牵到一座很漂亮的偏殿中，精心饲养起来。从此这马食则精草细料，饮则甘泉之水，既不用为追草逐水奔波，也不必为驾车耕田担忧，长得膘肥肉满，心中得意极了。谁知好景不长，有一次黄帝又要出巡天下，正要召六龙来驾车，旁边有个臣子说："我听说麒麟行如疾风行云，一时三刻间就走遍天下，大王何不乘那只麒麟出巡呢？"黄帝闻言大喜，命人将那匹"麒麟"牵来，刚刚要骑上去，忽然一阵风吹来，把马身上的麒麟皮掀起，露出四只马脚和尾巴来。真情已露，黄帝大怒，命人将马拴在马柱上，勒上嚼子，带上"过梁"，狠狠地用皮鞭把它抽了一顿。从此嚼子和过梁二物，便作为一种驯马的刑具，留在人间。不论多烈的马，只要一勒上嚼子，它的烈性就减去五分，再给它勒上过梁，那匹马就立时变得服服贴贴了。

　　后来，人们便用"露马脚"来形容隐私或阴谋的败露。

According to legend, during the reign of the mythical first ruler of China, the Yellow Emperor, all animals on earth, even the ferocious tiger and the hissing poisonous snake were tamed. When the emperor made his royal inspection tours of all of his land he would be accompanied by the phoenix and his chariot would be pulled by six dragons. The lion acted as the vanguard. Even the hawk flew overhead, flapping its wings to keep the emperor cool during hot weather. But the only exception was the animal that symbolized good fortune — the unicorn — who would not take part as it would not submit to the authority of the emperor. The emperor was unhappy about it and determined to have the unicorn become a part of his retinue. The horse learned of the matter and thought of a way to use it to his advantage. The horse then cunningly disguised itself with the hide of the unicorn and went to see the Yellow Emperor. The emperor was so elated that he gave the "unicorn" a beautiful side hall in his palace. He ordered that the animal should be fed with delicious and plentiful food. Thus the horse obtained fine straw for his meal and drank water from the sweet fountain. The horse no longer had to roam in the wild in search of fodder, neither did it have to pull the cart, nor till the land. The horse was living an indulged and privileged life. However, its good time didn't last long.

The emperor was preparing to make an inspection tour. He ordered the six dragons to pull the chariot for him but an official remarked that he had heard that the unicorn galloped as fast as the clouds and the wind and could make the journey in a much shorter time. The official, as fate would have it, suggested that the emperor should ride on the unicorn. The emperor summoned the "unicorn", and just as the emperor was about to mount it, the wind blew up a corner of the unicorn hide and the cloven hooves and the tail of the horse were revealed. The emperor was infuriated and ordered the horse to be punished. The horse was whipped many times and a mouth brace attached to reins were inflicted upon the horse to restrict its freedom. Since then, this method has been used to tame horses. No matter how wild a horse may be if you pull on the reins and whip it under the brace, the horse will become obedient.

Subsequently, people use the phrase "show the cloven hooves" as an expression to describe betraying one's own identity or to describe the exposure of an intrigue.

马 马 虎 虎
mǎ　mǎ　hu　hu

TO BE SLOPPY

马马和虎虎自幼相好,虽然都已成家,仍然你来我往,非常亲密。

一天马马到虎虎家去玩,走进大门,见虎虎的妻子正在院里梳头,而虎虎则上街赶集去了。马马在屋里看了会儿书,见虎虎还不回来,就出来说:"我改日再来。"虎虎的妻再三挽留,马马不肯,出门走了。

虎妻梳完头,发现头上插的金簪子不见了。她想:刚才除了马大哥来过,没有别人进来呀。这时虎虎回来了,虎妻说:"刚才马大哥找你玩,见你不在家,他就走了。"又说道:"你说怪不怪。刚才我梳头时把金簪子放在门墩上,可梳完头却再也找不到了,不是马大哥顺手拿走了吧?"虎虎哈哈一笑说:"不会,不会,找不着就算了,明儿上街再买一个。"

过了两天,马马又来玩,虎虎因为几天没见马马了,分外热情。两人谈古论今,笑声不止。这时虎妻进来添茶,随口说道:"马大哥,你看多怪,上回你来,我在梳头,后来金簪子不见了,是不是你顺手拿走了?"马马一听,心想她丢了金簪子,可是并不是我拿的,怎么办呢?为了朋友之情,说个假话,含糊过去算了,以后定会弄清楚的。想到这里,他一拍腿说:"看我记性多坏,上次我看弟妹的簪子好,就拿回去给你嫂嫂试试,今天忘了带来,下次一定带来。"虎妻一听高兴极了,说:"这下我可放心了。"

这天马马回到家里,唉声叹气,坐立不安。妻子连连追问,马马只好讲了原由。妻子听后,心里思忖一下,进屋拿出自己的钱和一些首饰,让马马上街当了,买了个金簪子给弟妹送去。

马马拿着金簪子来到虎虎家,交给虎妻说:"原来那个,你嫂子不小心弄丢了,我想反正在屋里,迟早会找到的,就给你买了个新的。"虎妻推辞不过,只好收下了。接着,她又对虎虎说:"咱家那只大母鸭成天不下蛋,你把它杀了,招待马大哥。"

虎虎杀死鸭子剖开膛,忽然看见一个金簪子滑了出来。他感到非常惊讶,急忙叫妻子来看,原来是鸭子吞了金簪子。两人慌忙告诉马马。马马见原簪子找到了,顿时放了心。那天,马马在虎虎家玩到天黑才回家。

马马走后,虎虎夫妻甚觉不安。虎虎对妻子说:"像马大哥、马大嫂这样的好人,世上真是少有啊!我想,咱家有这样多的财产,不如把他们接过来,两家合为一家,你看怎样?"妻子一听,十分乐意。

接着,虎虎夫妻便把马马夫妻接了过来,两家合户,过着非常和睦的日子。据说过了许多代,他们的子孙仍然没有分家。他们的后代在村中行走的时候,村里的人连他们当中谁姓马,谁姓虎也分辨不清。每逢这时,人们就说:"马马虎虎过去算了。"从此以后,"马马虎虎"这个俗语就流传开来。直到今天人们仍然用它形容做事不认真,精心大意。有时也用来形容生活过得还可以。

Mama and Huhu grew up together and were always the best of friends. Even after they got married and each had his own home, they were still the best of buddies.

One day Mama called on Huhu at his home. He saw the wife of Huhu was combing her hair in the courtyard, but Huhu had gone to the market. He waited for a while but Huhu was still not back so he told Huhu's wife he would visit some other time and then he departed.

Huhu's wife finished combing her hair and found her golden hairpin was missing. No one had come to the house but Mama. Huhu returned and she told him that Mama had come to see him. She then told him that she was a little vexed because she had left her hairpin on the stone block at the side of door steps of the house and after Mama had left she couldn't find it. She speculated as to whether it was Mama who had taken it but Huhu said he doubted this and reassured his wife not to worry and that he would buy her a new hairpin.

A few days later Mama returned to visit his friend. The two engaged in a long conversation about many topics from the very ancient to the present day. They laughed and chatted as old friends do. When Huhu's wife came in and added hot water to their tea, she said, "Elder brother Ma, do you remember the other day when you came to our house and I was combing my hair? Well, after you left I couldn't find my hairpin, did you borrow it?" Mama felt that for the sake of his friendship with Huhu he should tell a white lie and say he took it to avoid further speculation. The truth can come out later on. So he said, in a confused manner, as he patted his leg, "I saw it was a good hairpin. I took it home to see if my wife liked it but I have forgotten to bring it with me today. I shall give it back to you the next time I come." The wife of Huhu was relieved to have her hairpin found and said so to Mama.

Mama was very uneasy, he returned home and his wife hearing him sigh asked what was the matter. Mama told her all about it. The wife thought about the matter, then she went into the house, took out some of her own money and asked her husband to pawn her ornaments and buy a hairpin for the wife of Huhu.

Mama bought a new hairpin, he gave it to Huhu's wife and told her that the original hairpin had been lost somewhere in the house. Huhu's wife declined but Mama insisted. That night Huhu and his wife entertained Mama to a delicious dinner of roast duck. When Huhu cut open the chest of the duck he found a gold hairpin in its breast. He realized that this was his wife's hairpin and they told Mama at once that he had been covering up for a duck. Mama was relieved that the truth had finally come out. Mama and Huhu spent the day together as content in each other's company as ever. However, Huhu's wife was still a little uneasy about the matter. She believed Mama and his wife to be good people, especially for offering the hairpin when they did not have very much money. She then suggested that Mama and his wife come to live with them, as they have plenty of money. She was very excited to think the two families could be united into one big happy family.

Mama and his wife moved in with Huhu and his wife. They registered themselves as members of one family and lived in contentment. Even their descendants never separated from each other and carried on a joint family partnership. When the Mama's or the Huhu's walked in the street people could not tell whether it was a Ma or a Hu. Then the people decided to just say that is Mamahuhu who had come.

This name has become a popular saying that has spread far and wide among the people. Due to Mama's roundabout way of solving a problem and people settling on the name mamahuhu because it was too hard to differentiate between the two, the name has come to denote doing things carelessly, with negligence, or lacking in conscientiousness. It can also mean so-so when asked about "How's business?" or "How are you getting along?"

效 犬 马 之 劳

xiào   quǎn   mǎ   zhī   láo

RENDER THE SERVICE OF A DOG AND A HORSE

　　相传,从前有一个人特别喜欢他养的那条狗,到哪儿去都领着它。有一次他到朋友家去赴宴,自然也少不了带着他的爱犬。虽然不让它坐上席,也免不了在桌下捡点骨头鱼刺吃。

　　席散后,狗会领着喝醉酒的主人往家走。半途中被风一吹,主人的酒性发作,跌倒在路旁一堆柴草上,不省人事了。这狗就蹲在身旁耐心守候。一会儿,草堆起火,风助火势,眼看就要烧到柴草堆上了,狗急得汪汪直叫,却一直叫不醒主人。于是,它就用舌头舔主人的脸,用爪子搬他的头,都没有用。这狗灵机一动,跳到附近的水池里,浸了一身水,在草堆上连爬带滚,然后又跳进水里,来回折腾了老半天,柴草全滚湿了,火烧到草堆前,也就自然灭了。聪明的狗,救了主人一命。

　　再说马。

　　古时候,有一个领兵的将军,打了败仗,单枪匹马,落荒而逃。跑到一座悬崖上,马失前蹄,将军从马上跌下崖去。挂在崖上的一棵柏树枝上。此时,上不来,下不去,后边追兵越来越近。在这危急之时,这马站到崖前,伸长脖子,顺下了马缰绳,让将军抓住缰绳,爬上悬崖,使他转危为安。

　　后来,人们根据上面两个故事总结出了"效犬马之劳"这句俗语,用来形容一个人对其主人忠心耿耿,甘愿像犬和马一样为主人效劳。

This is a story of a man who loves his dog and a dog who is devoted to his master. This man and dog were excellent companions and went everywhere together. On a day like any other, the man attended a friend's party. He fed some meat and fish bones to his dog sitting at his feet under the dinner table.

After the dinner party, the man, who was rather drunk, set off for home with the dog leading the way. The intoxicated man was blown by a gust of wind and lost his balance. Collapsing onto a pile of straw by the roadside, he became unconscious. Suddenly a fire broke out. Fuelled by the wind, the fire spread rapidly. The dog barked to get the attention of his master but he would not wake up. The dog licked its master's face and used its claws to move his head to try to wake him up. But the dog's efforts were in vain. Finally, the dog jumped into a pond, and then rolled on the straw with its saturated fur until the straw became wet. The dog did this several times until the straw became soaked with water and the fire was extinguished. The clever dog had successfully saved the life of its master.

The story now moves to the dedication of a horse. Long ago, a general was defeated in a battle and had to flee. He was alone and making his escape through the wilderness. When the general came to a precipice, his horse slipped and he fell from the cliff. He was caught by the branch of a tree. It was a dangerous moment as the enemy was approaching. The horse stretched its long neck and lowered its reins to the general so that he could climb up to the cliff. He made it up the cliff and escaped the enemy.

These two miraculous stories later gave rise to the saying "render the service of a dog and a horse," which is used to describe one who serves his master faithfully.

目 不 识 丁

mù　　bù　　shí　　dīng

DO NOT EVEN RECOGNIZE
THE CHARACTER *DING*

从前有个姓丁的财主,他有个儿子,十多岁了,还傻得厉害;丁家请了几个先生,也没教会他一个字。财主急了,贴出榜文:谁能教会少爷一个字,赏银十两。

　　一位老秀才揭了榜,到丁家当了先生。他想:"这孩子再笨,总不致于连自己的姓都不认识吧?何况"丁"字既好写,又好认,只一横一竖钩,我先教会他个"丁"字。于是他便写下个"丁"字,教少爷念了整整九天。到了第十天,财主要考考少爷,看看先生教会他几个字了。先生怕少爷忘了,特意准备了一个钉子让少爷拿着,再三叮咛:"你要忘了那个字,看看手里拿的钉子,准能想起来。"

　　先生领少爷去见财主,写下一个"丁"字,说:"少爷,快给老爷念念这个字!"

　　谁知少爷看了半天,也想不起是什么字了。先生赶快提醒他:"你手里拿的是什么?"

　　少爷看了看手中的钉子,连忙说:"这是铁棍。"

　　先生跺着脚说:"朽木不可雕也!你目不识丁不要紧,我那十两银子也拿不到了!"

　　后来,人们用"目不识丁"形容一个字也不识的人。

A long time ago there lived a man named Ding who was very rich but his son was very dumb. The father employed tutors to teach the boy to read and write, but no one succeeded. With no other option, the father issued a public notice promising to reward ten taels of silver to anyone who could teach his son to remember one word.

An old scholar took up the challenge in the hope that he might reap the reward. He decided to teach the boy the character "*ding*", which was his surname. He thought the boy could surely remember that even though he was such a dumb boy. The character "*ding*" only requires one horizontal stroke and another vertical one with a slash to the left. He wrote "*ding*" on a piece of paper and asked his student to memorize it. The boy practiced for nine whole days. On the tenth day, the rich man summoned his son to test him. As the Chinese character meaning iron nail is also pronounced "*ding*", the tutor took out three iron nails to remind the boy of the character "*ding*" which was his surname. The tutor hoped when his father questioned him he could look at the nails and recall the character "*ding*".

The tutor took the boy to his father. He wrote "*ding*" on a piece of paper and asked the boy to read and pronounce it. The boy held the nail in his hand but simply could not remember the word "*ding*". The tutor reminded the boy that it was what he was holding in his hand. The boy replied, "Oh, its an iron stick."

The tutor stamped his foot in frustration, saying that the boy was a hopeless case and that rotten wood cannot be carved into fine furniture. He said he did not care that the boy could not remember the word "*ding*" but he was annoyed that he would not receive his ten taels of silver.

This story later gave rise to the phrase "do not even recognize the character '*ding*'," which has become an appropriate description for those who are totally illiterate.

走 马 观 花
zǒu   mǎ   guān   huā

GALLOPING ON HORSE TO
SEE A FLOWER

唐代长安城南有个富家子弟,人称钱二公子,因为生就一条跛腿,所以三十多岁了还没有娶亲。城北孙员外家的三小姐,也因一张豁嘴,二十七八了还没有寻到婆家。

　　这几天钱孙两家都先后找到了以说媒为业的李大娘家,央求她给想想办法。这李大娘有心想给他二人撮合一下,但又担心他们双方互相挑剔对方的残缺。当时正好有个叫孟郊(751-814)的诗人写了一首名为"登科后"的诗,其中的"春风得意马蹄疾,一日看尽长安花",特别为人津津乐道。李大娘从诗中受到启发,决定施一"走马观花"之计,促成钱、孙二家的姻缘。

　　李大娘来到钱家,在钱二公子面前把孙三小姐吹了个天花乱坠,直吹得钱二公子恨不得立即把孙三小姐娶来,但一想到自己的跛腿,心里就凉了半截。李大娘见状,忙在他耳边献上了一条"走马"妙计。钱二公子听后连声叫好,赶忙让管家给李大娘一锭银子作酬劳。

　　李大娘又来到孙家,在孙三小组面前把钱二公子瞎吹了一通。孙三小姐听后心花怒放,但她刚一开口就犹豫起来。李大娘趁机又给她献上一条"观花"之策。孙三小姐立即拔下头上金钗塞进李大娘手中。

　　相亲那天,钱二公子骑在高头大马上,风度翩翩地经过孙家门前,只见伫立在门前的孙三小姐手持鲜花正在嗅香味。因为跛腿、豁嘴掩饰得巧妙,双方都十分满意。

　　经李大娘几次往返,两人很快就定下了迎娶吉日。洞房花烛之夜,等双方互见残缺时为时已晚,只好各自认命。

　　现在,人们就把那些只对事物进行粗略观察,而不进行深入研究的现象,称为"走马观花"。

In the Tang Dynasty there lived a rich man by the name of Qian whose second son Qian Er was crippled. Another rich man by the name of Sun had a third daughter who had a harelipped mouth. The son was over 30 years of age while the daughter was more than 28. No one wanted to marry either the son or the daughter on account of their deformity.

The two families had each separately asked Aunty Li, who was a professional matchmaker, to find a spouse for their son and daughter. Li had the intention to marry the crippled son to the harelipped daughter. However she feared that either party would pick the fault of the other and so she had to think of a way around this.

The matchmaker recalled two lines in a poem written by the poet Meng Jiao (751-814) entitled "Successful at the Civil Service Exam", "Successful; my horse runs faster in vernal breeze; I've seen within one day all flowers on Chang'an trees."* This verse described the happiness of a successful candidate. It inspired the matchmaker. She was determined to successfully unite the two rich men's children in wedlock. She went to the house of Qian and praised the beauty of Miss Sun. This aroused the passion of Qian Er, who greatly desired to make her his wife but he was concerned about his own crippled leg. Aunty Li told him of her plan for him to gallop on horseback so that Miss Sun would not be able to see his defect. He was so pleased with the idea that he asked his family steward to reward Li with a silver ingot for her pains. Aunty Li went to Miss Sun and praised the handsome appearance of Mr. Qian Er. Miss Sun was quite excited to hear about her future spouse but was hesitant because of her harelip. Li told her of an ingenious way to hide her disfig-

* The English translation comes from *Song of the Immortals* by Xu Yuanzhong.

41

uration, she suggested that as her suitor was riding past she could smell flowers which would hide her harelip. Miss Sun gave a golden hairpin to Li for her clever scheme.

The first encounter between the two betrothed was as follows. Qian Er rode on a tall horse and passed the house of Miss Sun, whom he saw was smelling her flowers on her door step and thus the harelip and the crippled leg were disguised. Both parties expressed satisfaction with each other.

Aunty Li continued with her work of persuasion after this meeting. The two families decided to marry their son and daughter. On the wedding night the couple discovered each other's true form but it was too late for they were already married. They concluded that it must be fate.

This story later gave rise to the expression "galloping on horseback to see a flower." Nowadays people use it to describe looking at something, someone or a situation carelessly without in-depth investigation or scrutiny. The consequences are then the person's own doing.

洛 阳 纸 贵

luò yáng zhǐ guì

PAPER BECOMES
EXPENSIVE IN LUOYANG

西晋司马氏建都洛阳的时候，来洛阳求官的人比哪个朝代都多。在这数不清的文人墨客当中，有一丑一俊两个人最惹人注目：丑的叫左思，俊的叫潘安。潘安见朝中贾皇后专权，就变着法儿去结交贾皇后的兄弟贾谧。加上他出身名门大家，写诗作文落笔成章，文辞又华丽，所以不久就当上了著作郎的大官。左思出身寒门，人丑口讷，脑子又死板，更不会看风使舵，自然难于当上大官。

俗话说，人不可貌相，海水不可斗量。别看左思样子不好看，却很有才气。他写的《齐都赋》虽然花的时间很长，但经过反复推敲，文章满篇锦绣，气势宏伟。左思写完《齐都赋》，又准备写《三都赋》(三国魏都邺城，吴都建业，蜀都成都)。左思知道自己读书少，见识不广，别人做官都找肥缺，他偏偏请求去当秘书郎，就是掌管国家图书经籍，没权没势的小官。一天到晚钻到书堆里。

他没到过成都，就上门请教阅历丰富的名人张载，向他了解那里的山川地理，风土人情。邺城离洛阳不远，他就骑上毛驴跑去实地考察、访问。经过漫长的十年岁月，他终于写出了《三都赋》。

《三都赋》一下子震动了京都洛阳。大司空张华亲笔写了序，说它能与当年班固名噪一时的《两京赋》媲美，文采也不在张衡的《二京赋》之下，还夸左思是当今的洛阳才子。这一来，洛阳城中的达官显贵、士农工商，就连闺中少女，个个争抄《三都赋》，无不以先读为快。抄书的人越来越多，洛阳市上的白纸卖得飞快，纸商见有利可图，一日数次涨价。到后来，"洛阳纸贵"就成了一句俗语，一直流传到现在，人们用它来形容著作风行一时。

When Sima Yan founded the Western Jin Dynasty in 265 and set up Luoyang as the capital, many people came to the city in the hope of seeking official positions. Among the intellectuals two men attracted particular attention. Zuo Si, an ugly man and Pan An, a handsome chap. Pan An resorted to all sorts of means to seek the acquaintance of Jia Mi, the brother of Queen Jia who dictated court affairs. Coming from a family of prominent scholars, Pan was quick with the pen and talented in calligraphy. Soon Pan An won the position of Editorial Director of the Secretariat. Zuo Si was quite the opposite of the showy Pan An. He was an ugly man who was slow in speech and was rigid in his thinking. As the saying goes he could not see which way the wind was blowing. Zuo Si found it difficult to move with the times. Although he was a hard-working man it was difficult for him to get a high post.

The Chinese saying says a man's worth cannot be measured by his looks just as sea water cannot be measured in liters. Zuo Si on closer inspection was actually a highly talented man. Over the period of several years he composed a *Qi Du Fu* (an ode to the capital of Qi). Then he started to write *San Du Fu* (a description of Yecheng, Jianye and Chengdu, capitals of the three kingdoms Wei, Wu and Shu). At first he recognized that his knowledge was inadequate for such a challenge, and so he obtained the position of assistant in the palace library to gain access to many books. His position was menial but it helped him to write his book.

Zuo Si was dedicated to his task and sought out many avenues for collecting material. He had never been to Chengdu, and so he enlisted the help of prominent scholar Zhang Zai to gather research on the geography and customs of the people of Chengdu. Zuo Si also rode his donkey to Yecheng, as it was not far away from Luoyang. After over a decade of hard work, he finally completed *San Du Fu*. This fine work became an instant hit. Zhang Hua, the Grand Minister of Works, wrote a preface to the book, in which he praised the book as being comparable to *Liang Jing Fu* written by the eminent scholar Ban Gu. The Minister compared the literary style of Zuo Si to the style of Zhang Heng. Zuo Si was praised as a prominent and talented scholar of Luoyang. The book was in great demand and paper sales boomed because so many people wanted to copy the book. Paper manufacturers and dealers raised the price of paper several times a day. Everybody was reading *San Du Fu*.

The saying "paper becomes expensive in Luoyang" was derived from this story. Today people use it to describe overwhelming popularity of a literary work.

狼 狈 为 奸

láng   bèi   wéi   jiān

COHORTS IN TROUBLEMAKING

唐代有个叫赵大的商人，有一天出城去办事，天黑之后还没到达目的地。他心里很着急，就离开大路踏上了一条横穿树林的近道。

出了树林，赵大忽然听见身后传来一阵沙沙声，紧跟着就有一双毛茸茸的爪子搭上了他的双肩。他知道遇上狼了。赵大知道，在这种情况下，万万不能扭头去看，就不慌不忙地用双手抓住狼爪，脑袋往后一挺，刚好顶住狼的下巴，使它张不开嘴。

老狼被赵大背着跑了一阵，眼看将近村口，狼在他背上挣扎起来。赵大一生气，把老狼从头上抢了出去，老狼脊背着地，疼得嗷嗷直叫。赵大刚想跑过去再给它添上两脚，老狼突然坐起身子仰天长一声，周围立刻传来许多狼的吼叫声。赵大急忙向村头打麦场奔去。打麦场上有一垛高高的麦秸，赵大奔到那里，竟然一下子爬到了垛尖上。

群狼奔到打麦场上，吼叫着从四面八方向麦秸垛扑去。可是麦秸垛又高又滑，它们扑到一半就滑下来。只见群狼聚集在老狼跟前，一只短臂大耳的动物正向狼群比划着什么。怪兽比划完毕，群狼又一次散开从四面向麦秸垛扑来，不同的是，它们这次不是往麦秸垛上扑，而是扑到垛底下用嘴叼着麦秸捆往外拉。眼看麦垛一截一截往下塌，赵大吓得直出冷汗，他扯着嗓子喊起救命来。

村里有个早起的老汉听到村头的呼救声，急忙回村叫醒村民。村民们手持扁担、镢头、铁锹、镰刀，敲着铜盆，一路奔向打麦场。

群狼见势头不对，不顾一切地纷纷向树林逃去。那怪兽逃了没有几步，就被赵大赶上来捉住了。

正在这时，人群里走出一位白发老者，他看了那个怪兽，失声叫道："它就是狈，因其前腿短于后腿，不能独立行走，只好依附于狼，共做坏事。"

后来，这件事就传开了。人们把那些勾结起来做坏事的人比喻为"狼狈为奸"，一直沿袭至今。

During the Tang Dynasty there was a merchant named Zhao Da, he went out of town one day to do business. As dusk fell and he had not yet reached his destination, he took a short cut through the woods. He suddenly heard a rustling sound and then felt a pair of claws on his shoulder. He knew it was a wolf, he cautioned himself against looking back at the wolf and instead took hold of the claws. He held back his head against the wolf's chin so it could not open its mouth.

The wolf was thus placed firmly on the back of the merchant, who kept walking on. When they reached the village, the wolf struggled to free itself from the merchant but the angry merchant threw the wolf to the ground over his head. The old wolf cried out in pain. Zhao Da was about to kick the wolf, when the wolf stood up on its legs and howled aloud, sending a piercing sound to the air to alert all of the other wolves. Soon the howling of many wolves was heard from all over the place. Zhao Da quickly ran into the village and climbed on top of a pile of straw.

A pack of wolves soon followed and surrounded the pile of straw. Fortunately the pile of straw was very high and was too slippery for the wolves. The wolves all gathered around the old wolf ready for action. There appeared to be an animal which was instructing the wolves. The animal was very odd-looking with short forelegs and big ears. The wolves scattered, then turned and stormed the straw pile from all directions. This time they did not try to get to the top and instead stayed down below and tried to pull down the straw from the bottom. Zhao Da was terrified. He shouted for help at the top of his voice. An elderly man who was an early riser heard the cry of help. He beat the drum to wake up the villagers, who soon came armed with sickles, picks, axes and bamboo poles. They beat brass wash basins as they approached to try to scare off the wolves.

The pack of wolves retreated and fled into the woods. The strange-looking animal did not run fast enough and was soon caught by Zhao Da.

At this point an old man came out and saw the strange animal. He explained to Zhao Da, "This is a *Bei*. It has short forelegs and cannot walk independently. It must act in collusion with the wolves to make mischief and do evil."

The event became widely publicized. As people talked about the story they used the expression "cohorts in troublemaking" to mean collaborating with others to cause trouble.

人不可貌相，海水不可斗量

rén bù kě mào xiàng hǎi shuǐ bù kě dǒu liáng

A MAN'S WORTH CANNOT BE MEASURED BY HIS LOOKS JUST AS SEA WATER CANNOT BE MEASURED IN LITERS

从前，有个姓王的人，在朝中当官，三个儿子也都在外工作，两个大的已经娶了媳妇，只有三儿子还没成家。

　　这一年春节，王大人带儿子回家过年，见老伴年纪大了，不能料理家务，就想从两个媳妇中选个当家的。老两口商量，决定出题考考她们。一天，王大人叫两个媳妇到集市上去买货，叫老大媳妇买骨头包肉，老二媳妇买肉包骨头。两个媳妇带上钱，边走边想着公公要自己买的东西，到了集市上，不知道买什么才对。两个人手里拿着钱，不住地叹气。

　　这情景让东庄郝山家的丑姑看见了，就问她们有什么为难事，她们只好实话实说，丑姑说"这好办"，就让大媳妇去买二斤核桃，二媳妇买二斤大枣。

　　回家后，两个媳妇将核桃和大枣交给公公。王大人见两个媳妇都猜中了自己出的谜，不住地说好。大媳妇说是丑姑娘猜出的，二媳妇便把买东西的经过说了一番。

　　原来这丑姑是东庄郝山家的小女儿，长得又黑又丑，所以叫丑姑。王大人见丑姑聪明过人，就让家人快去请媒人，给他的三儿子提亲。

　　那时候，男女婚姻大事全靠父母包办。所以这婚事很快办成了，没过几天便把丑姑娶过门来。

　　王大人要回朝了，便想让丑姑当家，又怕两个大媳妇不服，就又出了一次哑谜。

　　这天早上，王大人对三个媳妇说："你们都回娘家一趟，回来时，给我要个纸包火。带个布兜风。

　　傍晚，大媳妇和二媳妇愁眉苦脸地回来了，说："我们娘家没有纸包火，也没有布兜风。"这时三媳妇笑嘻嘻地进来了。左手递给公公一个纸糊的灯笼，右手递上一把布面扇子。大家都说丑姑聪明。王大人当场吩咐："今后由三媳妇接替婆婆管理家务。"

　　自从丑姑当家以后，全家的日子越过越好。不料，朝中有个奸臣想陷害王大人，皇帝听了谗言，就出难题，要他在一个月之内将海水全都变成酒；如办不成，就是违抗圣旨，要杀头的。全家急得直掉眼泪，只有丑姑说："公公，别怕，明天您带我上朝，面见皇帝，我

52

自有办法。"

　　丑姑被带到金銮殿，文武大臣两边排列，好不威风。丑姑却一点也不害怕，她决心和皇帝周旋。

　　皇帝问："听说你有办法把海水变成酒，用的是什么方法?"丑姑说："变法不难，只请万岁派个人，先把海水用斗量一遍，看看共有几斗，我们将用同样的酒替换。"皇帝听后说："这海水怎么能用斗量呢?"丑姑趁机说："既然量不出海水有多少，我可就不能将海水变换成酒了。"

　　皇帝见眼前这个女子长得又黑又丑，却大胆机灵，便随口说道："人不可貌相，海水不可斗量。"并马上吩咐赏赐丑姑百匹彩缎，又夸王大人娶了个聪明的儿媳，给他晋升一级。

　　后来，"人不可貌相，海水不可斗量"这句俗语就在民间流传下来了，人们用它说明不能只根据外表来判断一个人是否有才能。

Long long ago, there was an official of the court named Wang who had three sons. All of his sons worked in places away from home, and the two elder sons were married.

One year Wang went home with his eldest son for the lunar New Year holiday. When he found out his wife was old and weak, he decided that one of his two daughters-in-law should take over the running of household affairs. He discussed it with his wife, and they both agreed to give each of the daughters-in-law a trial run.

Wang initiated the test as follows: he instructed the eldest son's wife to buy something with "flesh wrapped by bones" and asked the second son's wife to buy something with "bones wrapped by flesh." The two women took money from their father-in-law and headed for the local market. They were both puzzled by the riddle their father-in-law had given them. Holding the money in their hands, they wandered around the market thoroughly dumbfounded.

A girl from the neighboring village stopped the vexed pair and inquired after their troubles. This girl was so black and ugly that everyone in the village referred to her as Ugly Girl. The two women told everything to Ugly Girl. "Don't worry, it is easy," she reassured them and advised the eldest son's wife to purchase one kilogram of walnuts and the second son's wife to buy one kilogram of jujubes.

The two women returned home and handed the walnuts and jujubes to their father-in-law. The advice of Ugly Girl had turned out to be exactly right! Wang was very pleased that his daughters-in-law knew the answers to the riddles. He praised them highly. However, the eldest daughter-in-law felt she should tell the truth and said it was Ugly Girl who had solved the riddles. The second son's wife reaffirmed this story.

Ugly Girl was the youngest daughter of Hao Shan of the Eastern Village. On learning of Ugly Girl's aptitude, Wang lost no time in sending a matchmaker to the Haos to make a proposal for his youngest son. The marriage between Ugly Girl and Wang's third son was agreed by both families, and the wedding ceremony was held soon after.

Wang had to leave home for his work post. He wanted Ugly Girl to be in charge of household affairs, but was afraid that the other two daughters-in-law would not listen to her. Wang, therefore, proposed a new riddle for the three daughters-in-law.

One morning, Wang said to his three daughters-in-law: "You may go to visit your parents today. When you return, each of you should bring me two things: one thing is made of paper with fire inside; and the other is a piece of cloth that holds wind."

At nightfall, the eldest and second sons' wives came back with nothing but worried frowns. They said: "We didn't find any thing that fits the description of your riddle at our parents' home." Then the third son's wife walked in, with a smile on her face. She handed a paper lantern and a cloth fan to her father-in-law. When all the members of the family were praising Ugly Girl for her intelligence, Wang declared: "From now on, the third son's wife will take her mother-in-law's place to be in charge of family affairs."

Under the wise guidance and management of Ugly Girl, the life of the Wangs improved tremendously. However, there was a turn of events. A treacherous official was plotting to frame Wang. He had convinced the emperor to put Wang in an awkward position. The emperor requested that Wang turn all the sea water into wine within a month, or Wang would be executed for disobeying the imperial order. Everyone of Wang's family was distraught except Ugly Girl. Ugly Girl said to her father-in-law: "Don't worry. I'll go with you to the court to see the emperor tomorrow morning. I'll talk directly with the emperor."

At the palace, Ugly Girl was directed to the throne hall. The emperor received her sitting on his throne flanked by a number of officials. Ugly Girl was not at all intimidated, on the contrary, she was even more determined to contend with the emperor.

The emperor spoke: "I've learned that you are able to turn sea water into wine. What is your method?"

"It is not difficult," Ugly Girl said. "However, you must have the sea water measured first to establish the correct quantity, then we can turn it into wine."

"How can sea water be measured?" the emperor inquired.

"Since sea water is immeasurable, I cannot change sea water into wine," Ugly Girl replied.

Finding the black and ugly girl was so brave and intelligent, the emperor could not help saying: "A man's worth cannot be measured by his looks just as sea water cannot be measured in liters." Then the emperor rewarded Ugly Girl 100 bolts of colorful brocade and promoted Wang for having such a clever daughter-in-law.

Today people use the saying "a man's worth cannot be measured by his looks just as sea water cannot be measured in liters" to mean one should not judge a person only by his appearance.

丁 是 丁， 卯 是 卯

dīng shì dīng   mǎo shì mǎo

KEEP *DING* DISTINCT FROM *MAO*

丁是天干中第四位,卯是地支中第四位,虽然数位相同,但是干支不能相混。"丁是丁,卯是卯"就是出自一则有趣的历史故事。

相传隋朝末年,隋炀帝杨广在洛阳城里举行了一场大比武,燕山罗成夺得头名状元。监考官杨林见罗成人材出众,武艺超群,非要收他作干儿子。罗成不答应,杨林恼羞成怒,说罗成谋反,要拿他问罪。罗成的结拜哥哥瓦岗寨首领程咬金带兵赶来营救。没想到杨林下令将四门紧闭,把起义军和罗成困在城中的东岳庙里,程咬金也中了埋伏,被隋兵捉进了大牢。

这事惹恼了前来观看比武的沙陀国(今宣化)公主。她是杨林请来的客人,是来帮助隋朝平定内乱的。她见杨林欺人太甚,罗成年轻貌美,就产生了营救英雄脱险的念头。那天夜里,沙陀公主潜入杨林的密室盗出一支令箭,送到东岳庙里,要罗成他们赶快逃出城外。罗成是将门之子,精通军令,一看令箭就说:"公主,你拿的令箭是卯时令箭,可以到牢房救出程咬金,但是不能出城,出城须要杨林的丁时令箭,丁是丁,卯是卯,各有各的用途啊!"他这一说,沙陀公主第二次潜入虎穴,又从杨林密室中盗出了丁时令箭,才把众英雄救出了洛阳城。

以上便是"丁是丁,卯是卯"的来历。这句俗语告诉我们做事要认真,一是一,二是二,一点不能含糊,否则便很难收到预期的效果。

Ding is the fourth of the ten Heavenly Stems*, and *mao* is the fourth of the twelve Earthly Branches**. It is important that *Ding* and *mao* are not confused. The expression "To keep *ding* distinct from *mao*" will tell you why.

Legend has it that at the end of the Sui Dynasty (581-618), Emperor Yang held an imperial fighting-skill tournament in Lu-oyang City. Luo Cheng, a young man from Yanshan, came first in the tournament. Finding Luo Cheng was a handsome young man with excellent skills, Yang Lin, the officer in charge of the tournament, offered to take Luo Cheng as his nominal foster son. Luo Cheng declined the offer, which enraged and humiliat-ed Yang Lin. In retaliation Yang Lin made a false charge against Luo Cheng, accusing him of plotting a rebellion, and sent troops to arrest Luo Cheng. This news travelled to Cheng Yaojin, Luo Cheng's sworn brother and head of the rebel band in Fort Wa-gang, and he immediately set off with his troops to rescue Luo Cheng. However, when Cheng arrived in Luoyang, Yang Lin had the four city gates closed tightly and had pinned down Luo Cheng and the rescuing squad in Dongyue Temple in the city. Cheng Yaojin was captured in an ambush and was put into jail by the Sui troops.

The Princess of the Shatuo State (present-day Xuanhua) opposed the actions of Yang Lin. She had been invited to Luo-yang by Yang Lin himself to watch the fighting-skill tournament and offer advice on quelling rebellions. The princess did not

---

*The Heavenly Stems include *jia*, *yi*, *bing*, *ding*, *wu*, *ji*, *geng*, *xin*, *ren* and *gui*, which are used as serial numbers and also in combination with the Earthly Branches to designate years, months, days and hours.

**The Earthly Branches include *zi*, *chou*, *yin*, *mao*, *chen*, *si*, *wu*, *wei*, *shen*, *you*, *xu* and *hai*, which are used in combination with the Heavenly Stems to designate years, months, days and hours.

agree with the bullying of Luo Cheng, a handsome and skillful young man, and she decided to help him. When night fell, she sneaked into Yang Lin's secret room, stole an arrow-shaped token of authority and sent it to the Dongyue Temple. She told Luo Cheng it will help him to get out of the city. Luo Cheng, a son of a general, was well informed about the military arrows of authority. He said, "Princess, what you've got is the *mao* arrow. It will allow you to get into the jail to set free Cheng Yaojin but we cannot use it to leave the city. The signal to leave the city is Yang Lin's *ding* arrow. The two kinds of arrows indicate different instructions. The *ding* is quite distinct from *mao*." The princess heeded this advice and once again stole into the secret room and took the *ding* arrow. This then allowed Luo Cheng and his men to escape from the city.

This story gave rise to the saying "keep *ding* distinct from *mao*." Nowadays people use it to mean that one should pay careful attention to details if he wants to fulfil a task, otherwise the outcome will be hindered.

人心不足蛇吞象

rén xīn bù zú shé tūn xiàng

A MAN WHOSE HEART IS NOT CONTENT IS LIKE A SNAKE WHICH TRIES TO SWALLOW AN ELEPHANT

从前，有个读书人。一天，他看见路旁躺着一条快要冻死的小蛇，心想：自己是个书生，决不能见死不救。于是，他双手捧起小蛇，揣进怀里，带回家中，偷偷喂养。

过了些日子，小蛇渐渐长大，他每天都把它藏在自己的袖筒里。

蛇越长越大，无法随身带了，书生只得将它留在家中，结果被母亲发现了。母亲让他趁早放掉。于是读书人抱蛇出门，来到原来救蛇的地方，将蛇放下，转身要走，忽然小蛇开口说话了："相公救我之命，必当图报，来年京中开考，相公莫忘应试，定能功名成就！"说罢，小蛇踪影全无。

不久，读书人赴京赶考，果然考得了个头名状元。衣锦还乡，合家欢喜。状元来到放蛇的那个地方，对蛇去的方向拜了三拜，此时，只见树杈上倒悬一条大蟒，正在向他频频点头，并说："相公救命之恩，永世难忘。你虽然金榜有名，但朝里无人是做不了高官的。我的眼睛乃世上无双，价值连城的夜明珠，只要取我眼珠一颗，献给圣上，定可一人之下，万人之上。"一心想做高官的状元，听了自然高兴，但又怕蛇仙故意试探。于是他装出一副不忍心的模样说："怎能为我作官而让你受此痛苦？"蛇道："若非相公当初救我，我哪还有今日？别再迟疑了，赶快动手取吧！"状元当即上去，用小刀子挖出了蛇的一颗眼珠。蛇忍痛而去，留下一路血迹。

状元回家，用清水将蛇眼洗净，然后放在一只八角瓷盘里。到了黄昏，盘中之物熠熠生光，室内如同白昼。状元见此情景，高兴得什么都忘记了。

状元进京献宝，皇帝见了，龙颜大悦，知此乃神赐之宝，当即官封状元一品宰相。

状元觉得自己上面不光有皇上，还有王爷，王爷可以上骂天子，下打群臣，能当上王爷该有多好！可是苦于无晋爵良机。

有一年，皇太后得病，久治不愈。皇帝令拟一张皇榜，大意是："谁能治愈太后的病症，愿赐半壁江山，官封爵位一九千岁。

消息传出，宰相欣喜若狂，他告假回乡，又来到路边，求助蛇仙。片刻间，一条大蟒果真来到面前，宰相连忙跪倒在地，把为太后治病求药之事说了一遍。蟒蛇思索了片刻，终于说道："太后之病，唯我心上之肉方可治得，取我心肉，必须劳你进入腹中才是。宰相心里欢喜，有了蛇心，就可以成为九千岁了。他立即脱去袍帽，就朝蛇的腹中钻进去，蛇口早已闭拢，贪心的宰相很快就死在蛇腹中了。

这个故事发生后，因为"相"和"象"是同音异义字，"人心不足蛇吞象"的俗语，也就慢慢地传遍了四面八方。现在人们用它形容贪心的人。

One day a scholar saw a small snake lying by the roadside. It was freezing to death. The man thought: "As a scholar, I should never hesitate to save a life." Then he picked up the snake, tucked it into his chest, took it home and fed it without letting his mother know.

The snake grew bigger and bigger with each passing day. At the beginning the scholar tucked it into his sleeve and took it with him everywhere he went. Then the snake became too big and he had to leave it at home. His mother found the snake and she ordered him to free it immediately. The scholar took the snake back to the place he had found it. As he was about to walk away the snake said: "Since you saved my life, I should repay you. Next year, you must go to the capital to take part in the highest imperial examination. You will succeed for sure." Then the snake disappeared.

The time came for the scholar to leave home for the capital to take part in the imperial examination. He came first in the examination and was named Number One Scholar. When he returned to his hometown in silken robes, everyone of his family was very happy. He then went to the spot where he had last seen the snake and pointed three bows in the direction the snake had gone. Suddenly he caught sight of a big boa hanging down from a tree, the boa said: "I'll never forget it is you who saved my life. Though you're a Number One Scholar now, you will not be a high-ranking official as you don't have relatives or friends with status and power. My eyes are priceless luminous pearls. If you take one of my eyes and offer it to the emperor you will be appointed as prime minister, a man above all people and under only the emperor.

The Number One Scholar was eager to become a high-ranking official. However he was afraid that the boa was tricking him, so he feigned ignorance and said: "How can I let you suffer so much as losing an eye just for my promotion?"

"How could I be alive today if you had not saved my life?" the snake retorted.

As soon as the snake had finished its words, the scholar went up and took out one of the snake's eyes with a knife. The snake bore the intense pain and went away, leaving a trail of blood.

The Number One Scholar returned home and cleaned the snake's eye with water then placed it onto an octagonal plate. When night fell, the snake's eye sparkled, illuminating the whole room. The Number One Scholar was ecstatic.

The Number One Scholar presented the snake's eye to the emperor. The emperor was overjoyed, regarding it as a treasure given by the gods. He immediately appointed the Number One Scholar as prime minister.

The prime minister gradually became disgruntled. He thought: "How nice it will be if I was an imperial nobleman, who can curse the emperor and strike officials and officers!" However er he had no means for a promotion.

A few years later, the empress dowager was sick and showed no sign of improvement even after having been treated by many doctors. The emperor issued an imperial decree, which read: "Anyone who can cure the empress dowager's disease will be given half of the country and be promoted to be an imperial nobleman."

The prime minister was wild with excitement. He asked for leave and returned to his hometown. He came to the roadside again and called the snake. The boa arrived and the prime minister prostrated himself before the boa, telling him everything about the empress dowager's disease and asking for help. After having thought it over for a while, the boa said: "The emperor dowager's disease can only be cured by my heart. To get my heart, you must go into my belly." The prime minister was very excited thinking he would be a nobleman with the snake's heart. He lost no time to take off his hat and robe and crawl into the snake's belly. When the snake closed its mouth, the greedy prime minister died in the snake's belly.

This tale of the greedy prime minister spread far and wide. since the character meaning "prime minister" and the character meaning "elephant" have the same pronunciation, the saying "a man whose heart is not content is like a snake which tries to swallow an elephant (instead of 'a prime minister')" was derived from the tale. Today it is used to describe one who is insatiably greedy.

人 为 财 死 , 鸟 为 食 亡

rén wèi cái sǐ niǎo wèi shí wáng

PEOPLE DIE
IN PURSUIT OF WEALTH;
BIRDS DIE IN PURSUIT OF FOOD

从前,有个家资富足的老板,借东西必还,从不占小便宜。那年年底,伙计们聚在一起吃年夜饭。老板让大家仔细想想,有没有借人东西或者拖欠了人家银钱未归还的。伙计们齐声说没有。老板说:"一年三百六十天,我们天天到河里打水吃,可曾付过钱?河水来自大海,大海由海龙王掌管,吃水付钱,就该付还海龙王。"于是老板挑选张三和李四,把装满银子的布包交给他俩,即日启程,全部扔入大海。

张三和李四各有各的嗜好,一个爱喝酒,一个喜欢吃点心。他俩接受了这桩差使,都想:"老板真傻,有钱不花,却往海水里扔,实在可惜!不如留下来……"于是他们都打起了小算盘,动起了坏心思。

一个月以后,他们走到了海边。张三说:"总算看到大海啦,准备扔银子吧!"李四讲:"慢,我们还是第一次见到大海,应该先喝杯酒,高兴高兴。酒我带来了,你尽管畅饮。"张三似乎十分感激地说道:"我也早为你准备好了点心,让你快快活活吃一顿。"

这时候,两人坐在海滩上,一个饮酒,一个吃包子。不多时,两人都倒在海边上。原来李四在酒瓶里放入砒霜,张三也在肉馅里下了毒药,结果一起丧生。

老板在家里等候多日,不见音讯,又派出两名伙计,去海边寻找。

两个伙计日夜兼程,不到一个月就来到海边。他们找呀,不见人影,喊呀,也没有回音。后来他们在海滩上发现两具枯骨和几只死去的海鸟,旁边有个布包,里面四百两银子一个也不少。老板听了两个伙计的禀报后说:"一定是张三和李四见了银子都想独吞,于是你害我,我害你,结果白白送了两条命,真是'人为财死'啊!至于这几只死鸟,时至寒冬,寻食困难,见到海边有两具尸体,争相啄食,最后当然要中毒丢命了。这可以叫做'鸟为食亡。'"

后来,"人为财死,鸟为食亡"这句俗语就渐渐流传开了。

Once upon a time there was a wealthy proprietor. He never sought petty gains and always returned everything he borrowed. One year when all his salesmen had finished eating the grand dinner on the lunar New Year's Eve, he asked them if there was anything he should return or any debt he should pay. "No," all his salesmen answered in unison.

"Have we ever paid for the water we drink all the year round from the river?" the proprietor asked. "The river water is from the sea. The sea is under the control of the Dragon King. So we should pay the Dragon King for the water we have drunk." Then he handed Zhang San and Li Si a whole bag of silver and asked them to leave the next morning and throw the money into the sea.

Zhang San was addicted to wine and Li Si to snacks. Each of them thought to himself: "Our boss is a fool. Money should not be thrown into the sea. It is such a pity!" Each of them had his own idea about how to use the money.

After a one-month journey, the two arrived at the sea. Zhang San said: "Finally we have arrived. We'd better throw the silver into the ocean." "Don't be in too much of a hurry," Li Si said. "This is the first time we have ever viewed the sea. Let us drink some wine while we enjoy the vast magnificence of the sea. I've brought some wine. You may drink as much as you want." "I've also prepared some steamed stuffed buns for you. We may also enjoy a delicious dinner together," Zhang San said in excitement.

Zhang San and Li Si sat on the seaside, one drinking wine and the other eating steamed stuffed buns. Suddenly they both dropped dead on the beach. Each had poisoned the other: Li Si had put white arsenic into the wine and Zhang San had put some poison into the meat stuffing.

The proprietor waited for Zhang San and Li Si to return from their journey. A long time had passed, but there was still no news from them. The proprietor was very worried and sent another two men to look for them.

The two men walked day and night, and came to the seaside in less than a month. They searched everywhere for the lost pair. Finally they found the cloth bag with silver, beside which were two skeletons and some dead sea birds.

The two men returned home and reported it to the proprietor. The proprietor said: "Obviously Zhang San and Li Si each wanted the silver all to himself. Zhang San must have poisoned Li Si, and vice versa. As a result both of them lost their lives! We see that 'people die in pursuit of wealth.' The birds had difficulty in finding food during the cold winter. When seeing two corpses by the seaside, they vied with each other for the food. Finally they died too. This is 'Birds die in pursuit of food.'"

The saying "people die in pursuit of wealth; bird die in pursuit of food" was thus derived from this story. Nowadays people use it to mean that greed will lead to misfortune.

三句不离本行

sān jù bù lí běn háng

UNÁBLE TO SAY THREE SENTENCES WITHOUT REFERRING TO ONE'S OWN LINE

传说过去有一个县官，夜晚坐轿巡街，忽见迎面有个黑影一闪，穿入街旁一条小巷里去。县官疑是坏人，便命停轿搜索。差役从巷里搜出一人，带至官轿前。

　　那人是一个郎中，深夜出诊，遇到官轿，便躲入巷中回避，谁知被当坏人抓住，心里有些害怕，就谎称自己是去赶考的考生。县官说："哪有深更半夜去赶考的？"郎中答不出话来。

　　县官说："你既是考生，当会吟诗作对，我今出一上联，你且对出下联。"县官指着轿前伞盖说："黑柄双翎伞。"郎中当即对答："红丸八宝丹。"县官又指临街的一家绸布店的招牌出一上联："三尺天青缎。"医生不假思索地对出下联："六味地黄丸。"县官听郎中对出二联，心想这人才学倒不错，奇怪的是他为什么全用药名来对呢？于是想再出一联让他对。县官见远处一家高楼，灯火通明，窗中隐约可见一年轻姑娘正在灯下做针线。县官说："小女子头发光灿，必有三从四德。"县官刚说完，医生对答："大老爷面肤黄瘦，定是五痨七伤。"县官听郎中骂他，大怒喝道："胡说！"郎中说："胡说是热重，宜服清凉降火剂。"差役们听不下去了，一个差役骂："放屁！"医生说："放屁是下虚，要吃十全大补汤。"另一个差役骂郎中："要死！"医生一听转身就走。"你们老爷要死，我没办法医治，快另请高明吧！"说完，一溜烟跑了。

　　呆了半晌，县官恍然大悟：那人是个郎中。"真是三句不离本行啊。"从此，这句话便传开了。

Legend has it that one night a county magistrate was making an inspection tour of the county in his sedan chair, when all of a sudden he saw the shadow of a man disappear into a lane. Suspecting the man to be a criminal, the magistrate had his sedan chair stopped and ordered his attendants to search for the man. The suspect was then brought before him.

In fact the suspect was a doctor, who was on his way back home after having visited a patient at home. Seeing the magistrate's sedan chair, he entered the lane to avoid disturbing the official. It was to his great surprise that he was seized as a scoundrel. He was so frightened that he made a false report, saying that he was a scholar on his way to the capital for the imperial examination.

"What are you doing on the streets at midnight?" the magistrate asked. The doctor was stuck for words.

"Since you are a scholar," the magistrate continued his interrogation. "You should be good at making antithetical couplets. I'll say the first line of the couplet, and you tell me the second line." Then the magistrate pointed at the large umbrella in front of the sedan chair and said: "A black-handled umbrella with two feathers." The doctor gave the second line of the couplet: "A red pill with eight ingredients." Looking at a sign of a silk store, the governor said: "Three *chi** of sky-blue brocade," and the doctor burst out without thinking: "Six wei** of earth-yellow pill."

It was blatantly obvious to the governor that all of the answers were related to traditional Chinese medicines. Then he saw a high building in the distance. A girl could be dimly seen in a brightly lit room doing some sewing. Then the governor said:

---

* *Chi* — one *chi* = 1/3 meter.
** *Wei* — ingredient (of a Chinese medicine prescription).

"The girl with shining hair must be a follower of the three obedi-ences* and the four virtues.**" As soon as the governor had finished, the doctor replied: "Your Highness looks lean and hag-gard, must be a victim of the five consumptions and seven inju-ries."

Upon hearing this last statement, the governor flew into rage and shouted: "Stop talking nonsense!"

"One who talks nonsense suffers from inner heat. He must take antipyretics for clearing up it."

"Stop farting around!" an attendant cursed.

"Breaking wind means the lower abdomen is deficient. He should take some tonics," the doctor said.

"Go to hell!" another attendant exclaimed.

Hearing the word "hell," the doctor vehemently protested: "If Your Highness is dying, I can not save him. Please find a better doctor."

Suddenly the governor saw the light: "The man is a doctor. After all he can not say three sentences without referring to his own line."

This story gave rise to the saying "unable to say three sen-tences without referring to one's own line." People use it to describe those who talk shop all the time.

---

*The three obediences: in ancient China a woman was required to obey her father before marriage, her husband during married life and her son in widowhood.

**The four virtues: morality, modesty in manner, propriety in speech and efficiency in needle work.

三个丑皮匠，胜过诸葛亮

sān gè chǒu pí jiàng shèng guò zhū gě liàng

THREE COBBLERS ARE BETTER
THAN ONE ZHUGE LIANG

诸葛亮到东吴作客，为孙权设计了一尊报恩寺塔，其实这是诸葛亮要看看东吴有无能人。那宝塔要求很高，单是顶上的铜葫芦就有五丈高，四千多斤重，孙权被难住了，气得面黄饥瘦。后来寻到了冶匠，但缺少做铜葫芦模型的人。城门上贴起招贤榜，时隔一月，仍然没有人揭榜。诸葛亮心中暗笑。

那城门口有三个摆摊子的皮匠，他们面目生得丑陋，又目不识丁，人家都称他们是丑皮匠。他们听说诸葛亮在寻东吴人的开心，心里不服气，便三个人凑在一起商议，他们足足费掉三天三夜的工夫，终于用剪鞋样的办法，剪出个葫芦的样子。然后，再用牛皮开料，一锥子一锥子地缝成一个大葫芦的模型，在烧铜水时，先将皮葫芦埋在沙里，一试果然成功。诸葛亮听到铜葫芦浇好的消息，立即向孙权告辞，从此再也不敢小看东吴了。

从此，"三个丑皮匠，胜过诸葛亮"这句话一直流传至今。人们用它说明这样一个道理：一个人无论多么聪明，他个人的智慧也比不上集体的智慧。

During the Three Kingdoms period (220-280), Zhuge Liang, a military counselor of the State of Shu, once paid a visit to the State of Wu. Sun Quan, the head of the State of Wu, asked Zhuge Liang to design a pagoda for him. To find out whether there were wise people in the State of Wu, Zhuge Liang deliberately made a complicated design with a bronze gourd-shaped structure at the top which was more than 50 feet high and weighed more than 2,000 kilograms. Sun Quan was so worried that he became sallow and emaciated. Finally he found some skilled artisans, but they lacked a model for the bronze gourd-shaped adornment. Sun Quan had a notice pasted on the city gate to solicit the service of a capable artisan for this project. One month had passed, but no one had answered the notice. Zhuge Liang snickered to himself.

At the city gate there were three cobblers who were ugly and totally illiterate. They were called the Ugly Cobblers. When learning that Zhuge Liang had made fun of the people of the State of Wu, they were very offended. They discussed the matter for three days and nights and finally had a plan. They cut a pattern for the structure according to the way one would cut a shoe pattern, and then sewed a large cattlehide gourd-shaped model. Then they buried the leather model in sand and let artisans pour molten bronze into it. It was a success. When Zhuge Liang had learned that the bronze gourd was successfully made, he took leave of Sun Quan. From then on he dared not look down upon the State of Wu.

The saying "three cobblers are better than one Zhuge Liang" was derived from the aforementioned story. It tells people the wisdom of the masses exceeds that of the wisest individual.

三十年河东，三十年河西

sān shí nián hé dōng   sān shí nián hé xī

THIRTY YEARS IN HEDONG,
THIRTY YEARS IN HEXI

当年郭子仪平定安史之乱，南征北战，立下了汗马功劳，唐皇感激万分，便将公主许配给郭子仪的儿子，并为他们建造了金碧辉煌的河东王府。

正巧新宅添孙，双喜临门。郭孙从小娇生惯养，长大挥霍无度。等到上辈先后去世，门庭渐渐衰落，家产消耗殆尽，郭孙只好沿路求乞。

一天，郭孙来到河西庄，想到三十多年前的奶妈，便去寻访，庄前庄后的小户人家都问遍了，说不知道。郭孙很是扫兴，不觉天色渐晚，来到一大户人家，打听乳母的消息。门公道："老主人已经仙逝。"郭孙随门公走进院宅，一眼望去，只见粮囤多座，牛羊成群。正巧主人种田回来，一番寒暄后说道："家母在世时，十分勤奋，率儿女发奋创业，才挣得这些家产。"郭孙不解地问："既然已拥有如此多的财产，您为什么还要亲自劳作呢？"主人笑道："家产再多，坐吃山空；勤俭持家，则其乐无穷。"说得郭孙脸红耳赤，非常羞愧。

主人不忘旧情，挽留郭孙当管账的，哪知郭孙对管账一窍不通，天长日久，郭孙不禁叹息道："真是三十年河东享不尽荣华富贵；三十年河西寄人篱下。"从此这句话流传下来并成为一句俗语，用以说明一个人不论多么富有都只是暂时的，如果他不知道珍惜，总有一天会失去全部财富。

General Guo Ziyi of the Tang Dynasty was victorious in quelling the An Lushan-Shi Siming Rebellion. The Tang emperor, who was very grateful to him, betrothed his daughter to Guo's son and built the magnificent Hedong Residence for them. When the new residence was completed, Guo's grandson was born. Therefore, a double blessing descended upon the family. they were wealthy and had an heir. Guo's grandson was a very pampered and spoiled child and consequently he grew into an adult with no restraint. After the older generations passed away, the family gradually declined, the family property was lost, and Guo's grandson degenerated to begging for food.

One day he came to Hexi Village. Suddenly he remembered it was the hometown of his former wet nurse. She attended to him 30 years ago. He decided to look for her but to his disappointment, no one knew of his ex-wet nurse. At dusk, he arrived at the home of a wealthy family. The janitor invited him in, explaining that the old master had died a few years ago and the son was the new master. As soon as entering the house, Guo's grandson saw plenty of grain, cattle and sheep. At that moment the young master came home from field work. They exchanged greetings to each other. The master said: "When my mother was alive, she was very diligent herself. In addition, she taught her children to work hard. That's how we have earned our family property and I intend to keep it."

"Why do you still work in the fields since you are so wealthy now?" Guo's grandson queried.

"If one sits idle and eats all day, in time his whole fortune will be used up. However if you are industrious and thrifty in running your home, your life will be smooth and happy," the master said with smile.

Guo's grandson felt ashamed and his face turned red.

The master invited Guo's grandson to be his family accountant. However, Guo's grandson knew nothing about accounts. As time went by, Guo's grandson was very depressed, he said to himself: "During the past thirty years I enjoyed a high position and great wealth in Hedong; but in the coming thirty years I will live under another's roof in Hexi."

This story gave rise to the saying "thirty years in Hedong, thirty years in Hexi." Today people use it to illustrate that fortune, in whatever form it takes, must be appreciated, worked hard for and not taken for granted.

千里姻缘一线牵

qiān lǐ yīn yuán yí xiàn qiān

A FATE MATCH ACROSS
A THOUSAND MILES IS DRAWN
BY A THREAD

晋朝有个文人叫韦固,小时候聪明好学。他每天晚上一个人跑到郊外,在月光下背咏诗书。一天晚上,明月当空,他又来到河边,看到河边石头上坐着一位白发老人。老人手里拿着一个账本,账本上记着些人名,每两个人名中间画一条红线。老人边看账本边在河里找拳头大小的石头,然后把每两块石头用一条红绫系在一起。一连几个晚上,韦固都见老人在月光下系石头,心里感到好奇,就去问老人,老人说:"我这是给当婚的人牵红线,系在一起的叫婚姻结。这一对一对的石头,就是世上一对一对的夫妻。"

韦固听了就说:"那你也给我找一个妻子吧。"老人指了指不远处的一块小石头说:"它就是你的妻子,就是你这村东头看菜园子的那个女孩。"

韦固听了一想,那小女孩家里很穷,又瘦又小又丑又脏,心里不乐意,就将手里的小石头远远地投到河滩上,让老人给他换一个。老人却说这是定了的事,什么时候也不能变。

韦固回到家,一夜没睡着,总想那个小女孩将来要做他的妻子,他要倒霉,不如想办法害死她,这样就可以换一个人做妻子。

第二天清晨,他就去村东菜园子,见小女孩正在挖野菜。他拾起一块石头对准小女孩的头部砸去,小女孩被击倒在地上。韦固扭头就跑。他以为打死了人,不敢回家,便出了村远走他乡去了。

过了十来年,韦固考上解元,后来又做了翰林大学士。他年轻英俊,又有文才,提亲的不断,只是韦固看了没有一个称心如意的。

一天,有个朋友对他说,张老员外有个外甥女姓薛,生得十分美貌,琴棋书画样样精通,现在正在选婿。韦固听了心里有意,朋友就去拜访张员外。张员外也知道韦固的才华,只是要经外甥女自己看中才行,便决定次日请韦固到家中饮酒赏花,再作定夺。

第二天,韦固装扮得整整齐齐来到张员外家作客。饮罢酒,便来花园赏花。这时薛小姐同丫环也在园中,韦固见薛小姐果然美貌出众,心里便十分喜爱了。薛小姐见韦固仪表堂堂,也有几分爱意。张员外知道小姐看中了韦固,心中暗喜,当下就定了婚事,选定吉期。

到了大喜的日子，韦固将薛小姐迎娶到府上。洞房花烛之夜，韦固越看薛小姐越美，薛小姐不好意思地低下了头。这一低头，韦固发现薛小姐发根处有一块小疤记，一问才知道是她小时候被一个野小子用石头打的。后来父亲去世，她便和母亲住在舅舅家里。听了这些，韦固心里一阵难过，回想起小时候做的事，十分惭愧，便跪在薛小姐面前说："当初打伤你的就是我呀！"

随后，又将如何遇见月下老人的事说了一遍。小姐听了一阵难过。不过事已过去多年，韦固也知错了，就不再提此事。

韦固这才相信月下老人的话，看来姻缘是棒打不开的。

从此后，"千里姻缘一线牵"。这句话便流传下来，成了一句俗语。

Wei Gu was a scholar of the Jin Dynasty (265-420). In his childhood, he was gifted and studied very hard. Every evening he would recite poems under the moonlight. One night when he came to the riverside, he saw a white-haired old man sitting on a stone, holding an account book with his hands. On the account book were many names, each two names linked by a red line. The old man looked at the account book while searching for stones as big as a fist from the river. Then he tied two stones with a red string. For several nights running, the old man kept tying stones with red strings. Wei Gu was very curious and he went up to the old man and asked him what he was doing. The old man replied: "I am uniting persons in marriage. The string is the marriage knot. These pairs of stones symbolize couples that are meant to be together in the world."

Wei Gu asked him: "Could you please find a wife for me?" The old man pointed to a nearby stone and said: "It is your wife. She is the girl attending to the vegetable garden at the eastern end of the village."

Wei Gu was disappointed, because the girl was poor, lean, small, ugly, and dirty. He picked up the small stone and threw it toward the river. Then he asked the old man to find another girl for him. But the old man said: "Marriage is destined, and nothing can change it."

Wei Gu could not fall asleep that night, thinking he would be unhappy to have that dirty girl as his wife. Finally, he was determined to kill her, so that he could have another girl as his wife.

Early next morning, he walked to the vegetable garden at the eastern end of the village, and saw the young girl digging wild herbs. He picked up a stone and viciously struck her head. The girl fell to the ground and Wei Gu fled. As he believed that he had killed the girl, he dared not to return home. Instead he escaped to a distant county.

Over a decade had passed. Wei Gu passed the prefectural examination and came out first. Later he was appointed to be a Scholar of the Imperial Academy. Young, handsome and talented, many people came to propose marriage to him. But no-one satisfied him.

One day a friend came and said: "Gentleman Zhang has a niece. Her surname is Xue. She is beautiful and is good at music, chess, calligraphy and painting. She has decided to select her bridegroom."

Wei Gu thought Miss Xue would be suitable and asked his friend to go to the Zhangs to make a proposal. Gentleman Zhang knew Wei Gu was a man of talent, but insisted that it would ultimately be his niece's decision. So he invited Wei Gu to a dinner at home, and suggested that he might appreciate the flowers in his garden.

The following day Wei Gu dressed in his fine clothes and went to the Zhang's residence. After dinner, he followed Mr. Zhang to the garden, where Miss Xue was with her maids. At the first sight of her, Wei Gu fell in love. Miss Xue was likewise impressed by the noble and dignified young man. The date of the wedding ceremony was decided on that very day.

On the night of wedding, Wei Gu looked at his bride closely, finding she was more beautiful than ever before. The bride was so shy that she lowered her head and Wei Gu noticed a small scar. Wei Gu asked her how she got the scar. The bride told him that when she was young, a boy hit her with a stone for no apparent reason. After her father died, she and her mother came to live with her uncle. Wei Gu was distraught and ashamed, he threw himself on his knees before the bride and said: "It is I who hit you with a stone a decade ago."

Then Wei Gu told her everything about the old man he met under the moon. The bride felt a little upset for a while but she forgave him because it had happened many years ago, and Wei Gu knew he was wrong.

Wei Gu then believed every word the old man had once said that two people destined to marry could not be separated.

From then on, the expression "a fate match across a thousand miles is drawn by a thread" became a common saying.

不管三七二十一

bù guǎn sān qī èr shí yī

NEVER MIND THAT THREE TIMES SEVEN TOTALLING TWENTY – ONE

从前有一家大户,户主名叫李元。有一年,李元雇了一个五大三粗的长工给他干活。那长工初到时,李元对妻子说:"你每天管他三顿干的吧,免得他借去厕所的机会偷懒。"他的妻子照办了。那长工每顿吃三碗干饭,干起活来,一个能顶两个用。

隔了十天,李元又对妻子说:"这个长工干活虽然卖力气,但他的饭量太大了,一年要多吃我们几百斤粮食!从今天起,你一天管他三顿稀饭吧!"他妻子又照办了。那长工每顿吃七碗稀饭。干起活来有气无力,还不如一个弱女子。眼看稻田中杂草猛长,不抓紧时间除草,就要减产。李元心急如焚,想再雇一个短工,又舍不得花钱管饭。因此,他十分恼火。一天吃饭,李元责问长工:"你一天吃我三七二十一碗饭,为什么干活不像个男子汉?"

那长工边用筷子敲着碗边唱道:"干干干,一天吃九碗,周身汗毛都有劲,稀稀稀,三七二十一,脚酥手软如烂泥。我着急,没有力;你着急,有啥益?"

李元听了,想了半天,回过神来,当着长工的面对妻子说:"从今天起,管他三三九碗干,不管他三七二十一。"

他妻子又照办了。那长工干活又一人能顶两人用了。

这件事逐渐传开。开始,人们把改变错误的主张称为"不管三七二十一"。后来,将其含义慢慢引申开去,把不识好歹、不分是非的言行也称为"不管三七二十一"了。

Long long ago, there was a landlord named Li Yuan. One year Li Yuan employed a tall and strong long-term hired hand. Li Yuan gave his wife specific instructions: "You feed the hired hand three meals a day of cooked rice, and he is not to take unnecessary breaks with the excuse of going to the toilet." His wife did as she was directed. The hired man ate three bowls of rice every meal. He was full of energy and could do the work of two men.

Ten days later, Li Yuan said to his wife: "Although the hired hand works hard, he eats too much. He will eat several hundred *jin* (one *jin* = 1/2 kilogram) of rice a year. From now on, you prepare porridge for him three times a day." His wife followed his instruction. Although the hired hand took seven bowls of porridge a meal, he lost his strength and was as weak as a blade of grass. Weeds in the rice fields were out of control and the yield would be reduced if the weeds were not eradicated. Li Yuan was in a panic. He needed another hired hand but he begrudged spending money. The old miser was in a rage and he blamed the worker: "You eat seven bowls of porridge three times totalling 21 bowls a day. How can you work so poorly?"

The hired man beat the bowl with his chopsticks and sang: "With nine bowls of cooked rice a day, I am full of strength to earn my pay; but with 21 bowls of porridge a day, my legs and arms just fade away."

Li Yuan considered this carefully and he said to his wife: "From now on you feed him three meals of cooked rice a day, never mind that he was fed three times seven totalling twenty-one bowls of porridge before." His wife fed the hired man the rice and he regained his strength.

The expression "never mind that three times seven totalling twenty-one" was derived from this story. Over time its meaning has been somewhat extrapolated. Today people use it to describe those who make undiscriminating decisions without regard to the consequences.

无 巧 不 成 书

wú qiǎo bù chéng shū

THERE IS NO STORY
WITHOUT A COINCIDENCE

明代文学家施耐庵在撰写《水浒》时,有一天写到景阳岗武松打虎,怎么也写不好。他想尽用完了所有描写老虎的词句,总觉得不满意。因为他从来没有亲眼见过老虎,更没有见过打虎的场面。

正当施耐庵十分为难的时候,突然听到大门外一阵阵吵闹声,他放下手中的笔,站起身来,踱步到门口。

这时候,只见邻居阿巧喝醉了酒,正袒胸露臂地对一只大黄狗拳打脚踢,而黄狗则从各个方向冲着阿巧乱叫乱咬。最后,阿巧按住了大黄狗的头,骑在它身上,把它打得无法动弹。

这个打狗场面,给了施耐庵很大的启发。他想,武松不是也喝醉了酒吗?我把黄狗比作老虎,阿巧当成武松就行了。于是,施耐庵把刚才见到的打狗场面,着意描写了出来。回到房中,还把这事告诉妻子。他妻子听完后笑着说道:"真是无巧不成书!"(巧指阿巧)

后来,"无巧不成书"这个俗语便流传下来了。

Shi Nai'an (1286-1370) was a famous writer of the Ming Dynasty. One day he sat at home and wrote one chapter of *All Men Are Brothers* about Wu Song beating the tiger to death at Jingyang Hillock. He had spent lots of time describing the story, but he was still not satisfied because he had never even seen a tiger before, let alone a man fighting a tiger.

Shi Nai'an was suffering from writer's block and could not continue his writing. Suddenly, he was startled by a noise outside. He laid down his brush and looked outside.

It was his neighbor A Qiao who was rather intoxicated. He was fighting a large yellow dog which was barking and trying to bite him. Finally A Qiao overpowered the dog and beat it up.

The scene greatly inspired Shi Nai'an. When Wu Song beat the tiger up, he was also drunken. "I may take the yellow dog as the tiger and A Qiao as Wu Song." Then Shi Nai'an returned to the room and vividly described how Wu Song beat the tiger to death. Then he told his wife about how A Qiao gave him the inspiration. As the word "Qiao" is exactly the Chinese word for coincidence, his wife smiled and said: "There would be no story without coincidence."

Today, people use the saying "there would be no story without coincidence" to mean that the moments in life which are the most inspiring are often the most unpredictable.

太岁头上动土

tài suì tóu shàng dòng tǔ

BREAK THE EARTH ABOVE
THE HEAD OF GOD TAISUI

从前，没有房子的时候，人们都住地洞。人到哪里，到了一个地方，就在那里挖个地洞，往里面一钻，就算房子了。李老君是个能干的人，又会打铁，又会烧窑，手艺高而且心肠好。他看见大家都住在又矮又黑的地洞里，觉得实在不好，说："得想办法造房子住啊！"

大家一听，都说这个主意好，李老君就动手做，没过几天，砖头、瓦片就烧出来了。大家非常高兴，都来拜李老君做祖师，学造窑，学烧砖瓦。这样一来，烧窑的人就多起来了，到处烧窑取土，竟触犯了太岁神。

太岁神是专门管土的。以前迷信的人有个说法，谁家破土，就要翻翻皇历，挑选日子，免得碰上太岁神。谁要碰到他，不是生病，就是遭灾，所以有"太岁头上动不得土"这句话。

窑工多了，天天要动土，触犯太岁了。窑工们这个叫头痛，那个喊生病，李老君心想，一定要想个办法制服他。

正想着，太岁神竟找上门来了，气鼓鼓地说："李老头子，你叫你手下的人东边破土，西边取土，再不管教他们，叫他们赔个礼，别怪我不客气。"

李老君心里直冒火，但脸上不动声色，答应在窑上摆酒给他赔礼。

第二天，李老君摆了满满一桌酒菜。太岁神很是高兴，走进来后才看清楚，原来酒席摆在窑里边，窑肚子里烧着红彤彤的火，太岁神呆住了，那窑膛里热得吓人。但为了这桌酒菜，他坐了下来。

太岁神一落座，李老君在窑门口坐下，对外面高声喊道："生火！"

顿时，只见窑里火舌直窜，越烧越旺，把个太岁神吓得半死，酒菜也不想吃了，站起来就往外跑。这时，李老君把脸一沉，说："想走也容易，把话说清楚了。我们烧窑的，天天要破土，处处要取土，日后你碰到我的徒子徒孙，不准再害他们。"太岁神连声答应，李老君才把身子一让，太岁神一头钻出了窑洞门。后来，有人说太岁神的相貌很难看：头发是红的，面孔是黑的，歪鼻子咧嘴。那是在窑里烧的。

从此以后，太岁神只要听到窑工所用工具的响声，看到他们身上穿的黄围裙,就躲得远远的了。窑工要起棚造屋,种树破土,也从不问太岁。"太岁头上动不得土"变成了"太岁头上动土"就是这个道理。

后来,"太岁头上动土"这句俗语就在民间流传下来了。人们用它来比喻触犯有权势的人。

In ancient times there were no houses and people lived in caves. People were nomadic and would dig a cave in a suitable location and then live there. A man in these times called Li Laojun was very capable and was able to forge iron and bake bricks. Being a very kind man, he could not stand to see people live in dirty, uncivilized caves. He said: "We must learn to build houses."

Everyone agreed with Li and so he built a kiln, in which he baked many bricks and tiles to build houses. Folks came one after another to learn from him. To build kilns and bake bricks earth was needed, and so the ground was dug up every day. After some time, this offended God Taisui who was the ruler of the earth.

To assuage God Taisui, certain days were selected according to the almanac to break ground. This rule was quite serious because anyone who provoked God Taisui would become inflicted with illness or suffer disaster as a punishment.

However construction was well under way and God Taisui was already offended. Many people working at the kiln were sick. Li was determined to find a way to subdue the god.

God Taisui gave Li a severe lecture: "Your men break ground here and there and everywhere. If you don't stop them, nor offer an apology to me, I will be brutal and merciless."

Li was boiling with anger, but he pretended to be obedient. He promised to throw a banquet at the kiln and apologize to God Taisui.

The following day, God Taisui was pleased to see a sumptuous feast prepared by Li. However, he found that the table was very close to fire. The red flames from the kiln frightened the god but the food looked so delicious that he finally sat down.

As soon as God Taisui had sat down, Li pushed the god dangerously close to the kiln and blocked his exit, he shouted to the townsfolk: "Blow the fire!"

The face of God Taisui was lashed with the fire. He was terrified and tried to run away. Li blocked the way and said sternly: "We won't let you leave before we have an agreement. We need earth to bake bricks every day so you must promise not to hurt any of my apprentices from now on." The god nodded his head humbly. Then Li allowed the god to move away from the kiln. Burnt in the kiln, the god's hair became red, his face black, his nose crooked and his mouth broken.

Consequently, God Taisui would run away upon hearing the sounds of potters working and seeing their yellow aprons. After this event potters no longer needed to ask permission from God Taisui whenever they need to break the earth.

This story gave rise to the saying "break the earth above the head of God Taisui." Today people use it to mean provoking somebody far superior in power or strength.

饿 了 吃 糠 甜 如 蜜
è le chī kāng tián rú mì

饱 了 吃 蜜 蜜 不 甜
bǎo le chī mì mì bù tián

WHEN ONE IS HUNGRY, HUSK WILL TASTE AS SWEET AS HONEY; BUT WHEN ONE IS FULL, EVEN HONEY WILL NOT TASTE SWEET

刘秀在洛阳称帝之后，一切山珍海味，美味佳肴都吃遍了。有一天，他想换换口味。他想起当年逃难时吃的苜蓿芽糕，香甜可口，于是他下旨让厨师给他做苜蓿芽糕。

不一会儿，内侍端来一盘苜蓿芽糕。刘秀尝了一口，觉得味道不对，破口大骂，喝令把厨师打四十大板，赶出宫门。又过了一会儿，另一个厨师做的苜蓿芽糕送了上来，刘秀觉得还是难吃，下令把厨师押在水牢里。继而刘秀又命令其他厨师做，结果仍然与他过去吃的不一样。

就这样，刘秀不知杀害了多少无辜的厨师。有一位大臣实在看不下去了，就对刘秀说："万岁，您觉得上次做的好吃，何不派人把那个人找来？"刘秀连连点头令人把她叫来。

原来刘秀在落难的时候，被王莽追得东奔西跑，三天三夜没吃一点东西。好不容易甩掉追兵，躲在一个村庄时，已饿得走不动路了。他推开一户人家的门，里面出来一位白发老太婆。刘秀向她乞讨可以充饥的东西，老太婆面有难色，说家里确实没有可以吃的东西，只有一点苜蓿芽掺麦麸蒸的糕，于是把苜蓿芽糕递给刘秀。刘秀接过来，狼吞虎咽，吃了个精光。

　　过了不几天，老太婆被接到都城。刘秀见了恩人，令手下人殷勤招待。老太婆早就知道了刘秀的用意，想到因为自己给刘秀吃了一碗苜蓿芽糕而使许多无辜的厨师遭到杀害，心里很是难过。她对刘秀说："万岁，这苜蓿芽糕不要说是他们，就是我自己也做不好了！"

　　老太婆停了停，慢慢地说道："常言道：饿了吃糠甜如蜜，饱了吃蜜蜜不甜。你当时是三天三夜没吃饭，吃什么都香得很。现在你每天吃的是山珍海味，喝的是陈年老酒，再吃我们那粗茶淡饭，怎么能咽下呢？"

　　刘秀听到这里，方才恍然大悟。

　　"饿了吃糠甜如蜜，饱了吃蜜蜜不甜"这句俗语至今仍在口语中广泛使用。

After Liu Xiu ascended the throne (25) in Luoyang, he dined on delicacies every day. He enjoyed new flavours and cuisines every meal. Despite the constant supply of new and exquisite food, the emperor craved most of all to eat the sweet and tasty alfalfa cakes he had once eaten several years ago when he had been seeking refuge. He requested that the imperial cook prepare some alfalfa cakes to satisfy his hankering.

After the alfalfa cakes were presented to the emperor, he had a bite and found the taste thoroughly disagreeable. He shouted abuse, gave the cook 40 strokes of the birch, and expelled him from the palace. This was followed by the presentation of more alfalfa cakes by another cook. These were even worse and the chef was sent to the water dungeon. The emperor was convinced no cook in the palace was able to make alfafa cakes as delicious as those he had eaten before. The cooks continuously tried to please their majesty but it was all in vain and innocent cooks were killed one after another.

An official decided to somehow stop this alfalfa cake crisis from going on any more, he suggested: "Your Majesty, would it not be possible to invite the old woman who made delicious cakes for you some years ago to the palace and let her prepare cakes for you?" The emperor agreed and sent his attendants to fetch the old woman and bring her to the palace.

While Liu Xiu was waiting for the old woman he recalled the story of his alfalfa cake delight. Many years ago he had sought refuge in the village when he was being pursued by Wang Mang's troops. He had had nothing to eat for three days and was weak and ravenously hungry. Finally he had escaped from the enemy troops and entered a village. He was so hungry that he was not able to walk any further. He pushed open a door and a white-haired woman came out. Liu Xiu asked for something to eat, the old woman hesitated for a moment because she felt she had no food good enough for him but she had some alfalfa cakes. She handed Liu Xiu the cakes and he devoured them at once.

The old woman arrived at the palace. Liu Xiu was overjoyed and gave her solicitous hospitality. The old woman felt it was lamentable that many people had been killed because their alfalfa cakes were not to the emperor's liking. She told Liu Xiu honestly: "Your Majesty, I am not able to prepare delicious alfalfa cakes either." She paused, then explained: "As an old saying goes: 'When one is hungry, husk will taste as sweet as honey; but when one is full, even honey will not taste sweet.' Some years ago, you ate my cakes when you had acute hunger and believed them to be heavenly. Now you eat delicacies and drink wine every day, so it would be impossible for you to enjoy simple village food. I am sorry."

This was a profound insight from a poor peasant woman and a lesson for the emperor.

Today the saying "when one is hungry, husk will taste as sweet as honey; but when one is full, even honey will not taste sweet" is still commonly used in people's daily life.

吃 不 了 兜 着 走

chī bù liǎo dōu zhe zǒu

IF YOU CANNOT FINISH IT, DOGGIE – BAG IT

从前,古运河岸边有个不大不小的村子,村东头住着个六十多岁的林老汉,老伴早亡,自己和一个十六七岁的儿子一起生活。他从小在紫禁城里学了一招好手艺:蒸三鲜馅包子,为了维持生计,在门前开了一家包子铺。铺子虽然不大,但林老汉的手艺有名,再加上心肠热、为人好,所以不论是大运河里行船的,还是陆上过往的,只要从这儿过,都要到小店歇脚,买上几个包子,亲口品尝一番。有不少慕名而来的人,自己吃饱了,再买上几个捎回家里去,让家里人也尝一尝。于是林老汉想,不如做些小布袋,吃不了让人家捎着走。

第二天,他打发儿子到集市上买来白布,请人做了一些小布袋。

从那以后,林老汉每天白搭上几个小布袋,乍看上去,是亏了一些,但每天多卖了很多包子,便不吃亏了。顾客也高兴,真是皆大欢喜。

但是好景不长,这年春天,林老汉不幸身染重病卧床不起,不久就离开了人世。

儿子接管包子铺以后,开始仗着父亲的名气,生意还算红火。可是,没过三月,他蒸出的包子比以前就小了一圈。他对人说:"反正我的铺子名声在外,只要来吃包子,就给你端上十个钱的。"人家说:"我吃不了哇。"他回过身去拿起小布袋说:"兜着走。"人家没办法,只好把包子装进布袋捎走。就这样,没过多久,连布袋都不用了。干脆,吃不了的让他自个儿想法兜着走算了。于是,只要有人一进店,不管是老是少,是男是女,他二话不说,就端上来十个钱的包子,人家自然会说:"掌柜的,这些包子我吃不了。"他马上就答道:"吃不了兜着走。"

从那时起,"吃不了兜着走"这句话就传了下来,但意义有所变化。现在多用于警告或威胁他人时所说的话,意思是:你要对一切后果负责。

Long long ago, there was a village by the Grand Canal. At the eastern end of the village lived Old Man Lin and his teenage son. His wife had died many years ago. In his youth, Old Man Lin had learned how to make delicious steamed stuffed buns in the Forbidden City. To support himself and his son, he opened a small restaurant selling steamed stuffed buns in front of his home. In spite of its small size, the restaurant gradually became famous because of its delicious buns. In addition, Old Man Lin was a kind-hearted man and offered thoughtful service for his customers. Almost anybody passing by the restaurant (by the canal or by land) would enter the restaurant and taste his buns. Many people travelled from far and wide just to eat the tasty buns and take some home for their families.

One day Old Man Lin hit upon an idea: "I'd better prepare some small cloth bags for the customers who want to take buns home." He had his son purchase white cloth at the fair, and then asked a tailor to make some cloth bags.

Old Man Lin was thus able to offer his customers the convenient service of wrapping their take-away buns in the white cloth bags. The customers were satisfied and Old Man Lin was selling more buns than ever before.

Unfortunately this prosperity did not last long. Old Man Lin became very ill and died during the spring.

Old Man Lin's son took over the restaurant. At first the business was still good thanks to his father's fame. However, the son began to take advantage of the fortunate situation he had inherited. Three months later, customers found steamed stuffed buns prepared by the restaurant were much smaller. Lin's son thought: "My restaurant is well known anyway. I'll make a rule that any customers will be served 10 coins worth of buns and no less" and he did exactly that. He gave every customer the same quantity and if they said that there were too many buns he would give them a cloth bag and say: "Take them home." Soon he even stopped offering the cloth bags but let customers find a way, by themselves, to take away the buns they could not finish, that they did not want in the first place. Anyone who entered his restaurant would be served 10 coins worth of buns regardless. Old Man Lin's son would say: "If you cannot finish eating them, take them away with you."

This is the colorful story behind the saying "If you can't finish it, doggie-bag it." This saying was once used to mean getting more than one bargained for, and its meaning has somewhat changed with time. Today it is usually found in threatening words, as an equivalent of "you should bear all the consequences."

各	自	打	扫	门	前	雪
gè	zì	dǎ	sǎo	mén	qián	xuě

莫	管	旁	人	瓦	上	霜
mò	guǎn	páng	rén	wǎ	shàng	shuāng

EACH ONE SWEEPS THE SNOW FROM HIS OWN DOORSTEPS AND DOES NOT BOTHER ABOUT THE FROST ON HIS NEIGHBOR'S ROOF

　　从前有个人名叫葛志，在城里开了个杂货店。他为人勤快善良，乐于助人，生意做得不错。一年冬天，夜里下了场雪，天刚亮，他早早起床，为了方便顾客，冒着严寒，打开店门，打扫门前的积雪。扫着扫着，扫到邻居庞仁家门前，看到门旁瓦垛上放着个大箩筐。葛志走过去，把扫帚往瓦垛上一靠，伸手去端箩筐，一端没端动，往筐里一看，差一点吓倒在地上。原来筐里装着一具尸体。本来他平时就特别胆小，猛然遇到这事，吓得魂飞天外，他连扫帚也顾不上拿，赶忙躲回店里，坐在椅子上发抖。

　　直到天色大亮，葛志也不敢开门做生意。忽然听到门外人声嘈杂，知道尸体被人发现了。他蓦地想起自己的扫帚还丢在瓦垛上，连连叫苦。葛志正在害怕，忽然两个衙役闯入门来，用铁链子套住葛志的脖子，拉住就走。

　　原来天亮后，庞仁出来，见到尸体，直接到县衙报官。县官带人到现场一看，见地上脚印直通葛志店门，又见扫帚上刻有"葛"字，便断定凶手必是葛志无疑。

县官指使衙役把葛志押到县衙：立即击鼓升堂。葛志经受不住严刑拷打，只得伏罪招供，于是被打入死牢。

葛志的妻子见丈夫蒙受不白之冤，便到州衙鸣冤。知州为官清正，接过状纸看罢，觉得此案漏洞不少，立即传令县官查明此案。县官立即派人、四处侦破。经过明察暗访，终于使案情水落石出，真相大白。

原来庞仁的弟弟庞二、因与张三的妻子通奸，与张妻合谋用毒酒把张三害死，二人又移尸到庞仁瓦垛上，妄图栽赃庞仁。

后来，那些只顾自己的人劝别人少管闲事时，总爱用葛志作例子，常说："葛志打扫门前雪，多管庞仁瓦上筐。"天长日久，这话慢慢演变成了"各自打扫门前雪，莫管旁人瓦上霜"。

Once upon a time, there lived a grocery store owner named Ge Zhi. He was a diligent, kind-hearted man and was always ready to help others. His business was thriving. One day in the winter, it snowed the whole night, and the city was covered with thick snow. At daybreak, Ge Zhi got up, opened the door and began to clear away the snow in front of his store for customers' convenience. He kept sweeping the snow until he came close to his neighbor Pang Ren's door and saw a large bamboo basket in the way. He put down his broom on a pile of broken tiles, and tried to move the basket out of the way. The basket was so heavy that he could not move it by himself. He looked in the basket and was horrified to see a corpse. In panic, he ran back to his store and sat down on a chair, trembling with fear.

It was already daybreak. Ge Zhi kept the store closed and sat in his chair contemplating. He heard a commotion outside and realized the corpse in the basket had been discovered. Suddenly, he realized he had left his broom on the pile of the broken tiles and became very anxious about it. Sure enough, two *yamen* runners came, chained his neck and took him away.

That morning when Ge Zhi's neighbor Pang Ren walked out of his house, he found the corpse and reported it to the *yamen*. The magistrate and his men arrived at the scene and found footprints leading to Ge Zhi's store and a broom with the character "Ge" on the pile of tiles. They decided Ge Zhi must be the murderer.

When Ge Zhi was led to the *yamen*, a court trial was held. Under torture, he was forced to admit that he was guilty. The magistrate had him thrown into a cell for capital punishment prisoners.

Ge Zhi's wife knew her husband had been wronged. She went to the prefectural government office to complain and appealed for a redress of her husband's case. The prefect was an upright official. After having read the appeal, he had many doubts about the case. He immediately ordered the county magistrate to investigate the case again. After a thorough investigation, the truth was revealed.

It turned out that Pang Ren's younger brother Pang Er had an affair with Zhang San's wife. The two plotted and murdered Zhang San with poison wine. Then they moved the corpse to the pile of tiles in front of Pang Ren's house to frame Pang Ren.

Since then people who were of the opinion that one should not interfere into other people's affairs would say: "When Ge Zhi swept the snow on his own doorsteps, he should not have bothered about his neighbor's basket on the tiles." As time went by, this saying evolved into: "Each one sweeps the snow from his own doorsteps and does not bother about the frost on his neighbor's roof."

Today people use this saying to mean that one should mind one's own business and not poke nose into other people's affairs.

死要面子活受罪

sǐ yào miàn zi huó shòu zuì

TO UNDERGO A TERRIBLE ORDEAL
IN ORDER TO SAVE FACE

据民间传说，孔子有一个学生，写得一手好字，只是家里很穷。

有一年冬天，天下着鹅毛大雪，冷极了。孔子接到一家财主的请贴，请他去吃饭，然后还要请他写几个字。孔子想，不如带这个学生去。让学生写字，不是更显得我这个先生了不起吗？就叫这个学生一同去。

这下可难为了学生，去吧，身上的衣服太薄；不去吧，先生的话不敢不听。他的妻子想了个办法，让他穿了妻子的红棉衣，红棉裤，外面再罩上他自己的蓝布衫。这天，丈夫就穿了妻子的红袄红裤和先生一起去了。

这户人家的确是百万富翁，摆了一百桌酒，用的酒杯都是金的。可是入席时，孔子和他学生这一桌少了一只金杯。同桌的几个人为了表白自己，都撩起衣裳要主人搜身。这时孔子的学生非常尴尬。他暗暗地踢了先生一脚，孔子是个聪明人，以为是学生偷了金杯，如果搜出来岂不是大失面子，就站起身来说："好了，何必为一只金杯弄得大家扫兴，就算是我拿了。"说着，掏出十两银子作为杯子钱赔给了主人。

回来的路上，孔子责备学生，学生却说没有偷，孔子说那你为什么踢我一脚？学生这才撩起蓝布衫说里面穿着老婆的红袄红裤，怕别人看见，给先生丢面子。孔子听了连连顿脚："罢！罢！我十两银子买个贼做了。"

过了几天，那财主家派人送来一封信和十两银子，信里说金杯没有丢，是不小心落在雪地里，天晴雪化露出来了，银子是归还孔子的。孔子叹口气说："唉！死要面子活受罪，为了自己的面子，叫学生去写字，却差点戴了贼的帽子。"

后来，"死要面子活受罪"这句俗语就在民间流传下来了。

Legend has it that Confucius once had a student who was proficient in calligraphy, yet came from a very poor family.

One day in the winter, it snowed heavily and was extremely cold. Confucius received an invitation from a rich man that day to attend a banquet party. The host requested that Confucius dine with them and demonstrate his calligraphy afterwards. Confucius decided to bring his student with him and gave him the opportunity to demonstrate his calligraphy talent. He wanted it to be known that even a student of his could be a master of calligraphy.

The invitation put the student in an awkward position. In such cold weather, he did not have enough warm clothes to wear to attend the party, yet he was also afraid to offend his master if he refused his order. He became very perplexed. Then his wife suggested that he could wear her red cotton-padded jacket and trousers inside of his own robe. The student did exactly that and set off with Confucius to attend the party.

The host was very rich indeed. One hundred tables were laid out and all guests were served with gold wine cups. When the guests were taking their seats, one gold cup on Confucius and his student's table was found missing. Other guests on the same table flipped up the bottom half of their robes one after another to show their innocence. Confucius' student knew he could not flip up his robe because then everyone would see that he was wearing his wife's clothes. In an attempt to alert Confucius to the problem he gave him a kick under the table. Confucius thought that it was his student who must have stolen the cup. To save face, he stood up and said: "Let us not spoil our dinner over just one cup. You can just suppose I took the cup as a keepsake. I'll compensate it with some silver." Then he took out 10 taels of silver and handed it to the host.

On the way home, Confucius reprimanded the student. But

the student said, "I did not steal the cup."

"Then why did you kick me under the table?" Confucius asked.

The student flipped up his robe to reveal his wife's red jacket and trousers to Confucius and said: "I was afraid that the master would lose face if other guests saw my red jacket and trousers."

Confucius stamped his foot and said: "Oh, my goodness! I spent 10 taels of silver to make others believe I was a thief."

A few days later, the rich man sent Confucius a letter, plus 10 taels of silver. The letter read that the gold cup was not lost. It had fallen into a pile of snow, and after the sun came out and the snow melted, the cup was found.

Confucius sighed: "It happened because I tried to save my face. I tried to show off the talent of my student and, as a result, was almost mistaken as a thief."

The story thus gave rise to the expression "undergo a terrible ordeal in order to save face." Today it is still commonly used in people's daily life.

县 官 不 如 现 管

xiàn guān bù rú xiàn guǎn

THE POWER OF AN OFFICIAL IN – CHARGE IS MORE EFFECTIVE THAN THE POWER OF A COUNTY MAGISTRATE

说不清是哪个朝代的事了。有一天,县衙门口皇榜高悬,说是阳春三月乡试,黄金秋月大考。顿时,文人墨客纷纷聚拢,都想试试自己的运气。

说来也巧,县太爷恰巧大病缠身,眼看这个美差化为乌有,好不心痛,无奈皇命难违,只好将这美差托于心腹县主簿(掌管文书、办理事务的官)单淦。这位主簿跟随县太爷多年,见风使舵、阿谀奉承、欺上瞒下之行,无不精通。单淦这下真是久旱逢霖,如鱼得水,翌日就张榜招贤。

再说那些文人,有的苦读诗书备考,有的却以重金贿赂主簿。人人都想登榜夺魁。

时光如飞,不觉限期已满。单淦在后室看着那堆得像山似的钱财,正准备命人收摊卸牌,突然一驾四乘大车,载来一书生,说是要应招。单淦很是高兴。只见那人头戴方冠,身着绸袍,显然是个豪门弟子。单淦满脸堆笑,只等财神舍金。不料此人一毛不拔,好半天也没有拿出一文银子。单淦非常生气,脸色一沉,合起花名册,不再答理那人。

来人不甘示弱,问为何今日不报名了,单淦冷笑道:"进庙不烧香,心还诚不诚?"那人说:"我是……"单淦来了火,说:"哪怕你是皇亲国戚也不行。"那青年还是说:"我是……"单淦火冒三丈,喝令他滚,随即退到后室去点那钱财了。

这富豪子弟冲到县太爷家,号啕大哭,县太爷服药后,刚苏醒过来,看见榻前哭丧着脸的妻舅,不禁愕然,问后方知受到县主簿的奚落,不禁叹道:"往年你两个哥哥,不费吹灰之力送到上司,而高中官爵,如今你却在县主簿单淦手上通不过,真是县官不如现管啊!"

从此,这句俗语就在民间流传开了。人们用它形容直接负责某事的人,虽然职位不高,就这件事来说,他却比职位高的人权力大。

In ancient times, an imperial decree was published by the Magistrate of *yamen*, saying that a county examination would be held in spring; and a national examination would be held in autumn. Scholars far and wide gathered with the intention to try their luck.

It happened that the county magistrate fell seriously ill and was unable to retain his lucrative post as the president over the examination. He had no other choice but to entrust the job to Shan Gan, the county secretary. Shan Gan usually attended to legal, fiscal or secretarial duties in the *yamen*. He had worked for the magistrate for many years, and was experienced in all the tricks of officialdom; he was used to being servile to his superiors and tyrannical to his subordinates. Overjoyed with the new position, he immediately set to work the following day.

Every scholar was extremely eager to score well in the examination. To prepare themselves, some studied hard, while others tried their best to bribe the presiding official Shan Gan.

Time quickly passed and the day for the examination arrived. Hundreds of scholars registered and Shan Gan had collected a substantial amount of money.

Before the registration deadline, a four-horse carriage stopped in front of the *yamen*. A young man came out of the carriage and said to Shan Gan that he would like to have his name entered. Shan Gan immediately assumed that this young man, who wore a square hat and a silk robe, would offer him a good sum of money. But when he saw that was not the case, Shan Gan's cordiality quickly turned into anger. He closed the registration book and refused to have the young man's name entered.

The young man asked Shan Gan: "Why won't you enter my name?"

"Would you call yourself a devout Buddhist if you do not burn joss sticks upon entering a temple?" Shan Gan replied with a cold smile.

"I'm ...," the young man said.

"It doesn't matter who you are, even if you are a relative of the imperial family," Shan Gan replied sarcastically.

"I'm ...," the young man repeated.

But before he could utter another word, Shan Gan had him driven out, and walked into the inner room to count his money.

The young man rushed to the magistrate's residence, and complained bitterly to the sick magistrate, who had just waken up after taking medicine. The magistrate was very surprised to see his brother-in-law so troubled. When he had learned that the young man had been scoffed by Shan Gan, he said: "A few years ago, two elder brothers of yours were promoted to the rank of high officials with very little effort. But today you have suffered a rebuff from Shan Gan. This shows that the power of an official in charge is more effective than the power of a magistrate."

From then on, this saying has been used to illustrate that a person in-charge in a lower position actually has more power than his superior.

知 子 莫 如 父

zhī zǐ mò rú fù

NO ONE KNOWS A SON BETTER THAN HIS OWN FATHER

春秋时，越国宰相范蠡的二儿子在楚国因过失杀人，被判死刑，秋后处决。范蠡准备了千两黄金，让小儿子用船载到楚国，并写好书信一封，请他的结拜兄长楚国宰相帮忙。范蠡的长子不服气，对父亲说："这样重要的事为什么不叫我去？"范蠡说："你去不行，只有你的小弟去才能救活你二弟。"长子仍不服，范蠡拗不过，只得同意长子的请求。长子临行前范蠡叮嘱他，不管二弟得救与否，礼物不要带回。长子刚动身，范蠡马上叫小儿子去买一具棺材，到楚国去载二儿子的尸体回来。大家都认为范蠡做了一桩怪事。

　　范蠡长子到了楚国，拜见了宰相，呈上礼物和书信。宰相叫他将礼物放在门外，并盛情款待他。第二天，宰相启奏楚王："臣夜观星象见彗星侵犯紫微星，天上有灾难降临。王上只有即刻释放全部在押死囚，才能幸免于难。楚王听后，立即下旨大赦天下。

　　王榜贴到城门上，在被赦免的死囚名单中，第一个就是范蠡之子。范蠡的长子立即把船摇到城门下，准备接二弟出狱。路过宰相府，见黄金箱原封未动，心想：二弟已被赦免了，又何必白白丢掉这千两黄金呢！便命手下人把黄金扛回船上，便开船到城门口去了。

　　再说楚国宰相设计救了范蠡之子，急忙回府，准备宴请范蠡的二个儿子，门人报说：范大公子不辞而别。宰相下令快追回来，几箱礼物让他带回去。门人回禀，范公子已自己取回了。宰相一听，气得脸色发紫，说范蠡怎么会有这样没出息的儿子。马上参见楚王说：王上大赦天下，本为积德消灾，岂知有人说我收受范蠡一千两黄金贿赂，为了救出范蠡儿子才提议大赦。如放了范蠡公子，恐怕难平民愤。楚王听了说，既然如此，何不快斩了范蠡儿子，然后再释放其他死囚，岂不是两全之策？等到范蠡二儿子的头颅被斩下，运棺材的船刚好赶到。

　　范蠡为什么能料事如神呢？原来范蠡的长子是在他贫困时出生的，从小跟父亲一起历尽艰辛，深知钱财来之不易，而他平时又常见利忘义；而小儿子是在范蠡当官后出生的，从小挥金如土，一千两黄金对他是小事一桩，要他带回来，还怕麻烦呢。

　　后来，"知子莫如父"这个俗语就在民间流传下来了，人们用它形容父母对子女的了解之深。

During the Spring and Autumn Period (770-476), the second son of Fan Li, prime minister of the State of Yue, was sentenced to death in the State of Chu, because he killed a man unintentionally. He was to be executed in the autumn. To save his son, Fan Li prepared 1,000 taels of gold, wrote a letter and asked his youngest son to deliver them to the prime minister of the State of Chu who was his sworn brother. Fan's eldest son was annoyed. He said to his father: "Why don't you entrust me with such an important task?"

"You're not suitable for the job. Only your youngest brother can save your second brother's life," Fan Li replied.

The eldest son insisted that he should be the one to go. Finally his father gave in but before his departure Fan Li enjoined him that even if the gold could not save his brother he was not to bring it back.

As soon as his eldest son left, Fan Li asked his youngest son to buy a coffin and go to the State of Chu to collect back his second son's corpse. All who heard this were puzzled about his decision.

After Fan Li's eldest son arrived at the State of Chu, he went to see the prime minister and present him the gold and the letter. The prime minister accorded him with lavish hospitality. On the following day, the prime minister petitioned the emperor: "I watched the constellation last night, and found a comet was infringing the imperial star. It means that something untoward will be falling on Your Majesty. Only a special pardon of all criminals sentenced to death can avert it."

So the emperor issued a decree to that effect right away.

Then a name list was pasted on the city gate. The first name listed was Fan Li's second son. Upon learning the news, Fan's eldest son planned to have his boat berthed near the city gate to receive his brother. When passing by the prime minister's residence, he saw the gold was still there and thought: Since my brother has been pardoned by the emperor, the gold shouldn't be wasted. So he asked his man to load the gold on the boat and then headed for the city gate.

The prime minister of the State of Chu hurried back home as soon as he saved Fan Li's son. He planned to throw a party to entertain Fan's two sons. Then he received a report saying: "Fan's eldest son has left without saying good-bye." The prime minister asked his men to run after Fan's eldest son to let him take back his gold. One of his men said: "Fan's eldest son has already gone with the gold."

The prime minister was outraged and said: "How can Fan Li have such a good-for-nothing son!" He went to see the emperor right away and said: "Your Majesty decreed a special pardon for the people in order to eliminate disaster. However, someone has spread a rumor that Fan Li gave me a bribe of 1,000 tales of gold to save his son."

The emperor said, "If that is the case, why not execute Fan Li's son first and then grant a special pardon?"

Shortly after Fan Li's second son was beheaded, his younger brother showed up with his coffin.

How could Fan Li foretell what was going to happen with the accuracy of a prophet? It turned out that when Fan Li's eldest son was born Fan was very poor. The son suffered a lot in his childhood living with his father. He knew how life would be without money, and often abandoned all moral principles at the sight of money. However, Fan's youngest son was born after Fan became a high-ranking official and was used to the life of a rich family. One thousand taels of gold meant nothing to him. He therefore would not have taken the trouble of bringing it back home.

Hence the saying "no one knows a son better than his own father."

树 倒 猢 狲 散
shù dǎo hú sūn sàn

ONCE THE TREE FALLS,
THE MONKEYS ON IT WILL SCATTER

这句俗语的典故与南宋的奸相秦桧有关。

宋高宗时有个侍郎叫曹咏，因为善于察言观色、逢迎拍马，深得奸相秦桧的欢心，当上了朝廷大官，他家乡有很多人都来奉承巴结他。但曹咏的大舅子厉德新却与众不同，不向他献殷勤。原来厉德新是个头脑清醒的人，他知道曹咏是因投靠秦桧而升的官，料定这种人决没有好下场，不肯同流合污。于是，曹咏就暗中指使当地知县给厉德新施加压力，百般刁难，以迫使厉德新就范。但厉德新依然洁身自好，不肯奉承曹咏。

后来秦桧死了。那些因依附秦桧而升官的家伙接二连三地倒台了，曹咏也被贬至新州（今广东新兴）。厉德新听到这个消息，挥毫写了一篇赋，题为《树倒猢狲散赋》。文中将秦桧比作一棵树，把曹咏之流比作树上的猴子，赋中揭露了曹咏等靠着秦桧这棵大树的荫庇，作威作福，鱼肉百姓的行为。如今大树一倒，猴子四散。

后来，"树倒猢狲散"这个俗语就在民间流传下来了。人们用它比喻有权势的人物一垮台，原先依附他的人随即就散伙了。

This saying originates from the Southern Song Dynasty (1127-1279).

Cao Yong, a vice-minister in the reign of Emperor Gao Zong, was good at currying favor with his superiors. He was consequently favored by the vicious prime minister Qin Hui who promoted him to a high position. After his promotion, many of Cao Yong's country fellows came to flatter him, except his brother-in-law, Li Dexin. Li Dexin was a rational and sober-minded man. He knew that Cao Yong became a court official because of his relations with Qin Hui. He predicted this would eventually spell Cao Yong's doom and so refused to go along with him. Cao Yong was quite offended. He secretly incited the magistrate of the county where Li Dexin lived to urge Li to give in. But Li Dexin was proud and refused to change his stand.

Later Qin Hui died. The officials under Qin Hui fell from power one after another. Cao Yong was demoted to a position away from the capital, in Xinzhou (present-day Xinxing in Guangdong Province). Having heard the news, Li Dexin picked up his brush and wrote a descriptive prose with the title "When the tree falls, the monkeys will scatter." In the prose he likened Qin Hui to a big tree, and his followers to monkeys. He also exposed how these officials who won their posts through favouritism were prone to corruption and exploitation of the people. When Qin Hui died, his clique quickly disbanded.

Hence the saying "Once the tree falls, the monkeys on it will scatter." Today people use it to illustrate that when a man of influence falls from power, his hangers-on disperse.

清 官 难 断 家 务 事

qīng guān nán duàn jiā wù shì

EVEN AN UPRIGHT OFFICIAL
FINDS IT HARD TO SETTLE
A FAMILY QUARREL

从前有个县官,姓帅,由于他办事公正,深得民心,被誉为"帅青天"。一天早晨,帅青天刚上堂,皂役领来一个少年,哭告自己的妻子虐待老母,逼得老母投河。县官接过状子,详审一番,当即传令捉拿媳妇法办。

这时,帅夫人有事要请老爷。夫人说:"老爷办此案,务须谨慎。"帅青天觉得夫人言之有理,决定亲自寻访,再作定论。

原来那老婆婆有两房儿媳。大儿子在外经商,二儿子在家理财。大儿媳花言巧语而心肠狠毒,小儿媳不善言辞而心地善良,平日妯娌之间不甚和睦。待帅青天驾到,两房媳妇均在哭泣。细看那大儿媳哭得声嘶力竭却并无悲戚之色,而小儿媳轻轻抽泣却充满忧伤之情。帅青天心中先有了几分底。盘问之下,大儿媳诉说:"昨日弟媳将鱼渣丢给婆婆,难怪婆婆气得寻短见了! 小儿媳说:自己将烧好的鱼,挑选一条大的,取中段,剔去骨刺,送给婆婆,谁知婆婆认为是鱼渣,一气之下,离家而去。

帅青天听罢,又细访了左邻右舍,思前想后,决定提审大儿媳。大儿媳最终招供了。原来,那天大儿媳闻到鱼香,偷眼看见弟媳正细心剔鱼,不觉妒火发作,窜到婆婆房里,来个恶人先告状。 帅青天想,那小儿子又为何如此不明事理,诬告贤妻呢? 其中必有缘故。稍稍用刑,大媳妇只得和盘托出:原来她平日引诱小叔,暗通奸情,故使此伎俩,坑害小儿媳。

帅青天正欲拍板定叔嫂死罪,不想夫人在堂后大咳一声,他姑且退了堂。原来夫人认为老婆婆生死下落不明,定罪也应视后果究竟如何。恰在此时,大儿子搀扶着老母来到堂上,叩拜青天。原来婆婆奔到河边,适逢大儿子搭商船靠岸,惊问缘由,禀母道:"弟媳剔去骨刺,正是大孝,母亲您冤枉她了!说得母亲愧疚交加。

帅青天对老婆婆的大儿媳和小儿子分别给予恰当的惩处,使婆婆受到教育,对大儿子嘉勉,给小儿媳伸冤表彰。众皆叹服,都道:"这真是清官难断家务事,帅青天偏能明断家务事啊!"

后来,"清官难断家务事"这个俗语就在民间流传开了,人们用它形容家庭纠纷的复杂和难以解决。

Long long ago, there was a county magistrate, whose surname was Shuai. As he was just and upright, he was deeply loved by the people and was called "Shuai, the Blue Sky." One morning when Magistrate Shuai had just sat down at the court room, a young man was brought in by a *yamen* runner. The man cried and wanted to sue his wife for mistreating his mother and compelling her to commit suicide by drowning herself in the river. Shuai accepted and studied his written complaint, then issued an order to have the man's wife arrested.

At this moment the wife of the magistrate arrived at the scene. She stopped her husband and said: "You must be very careful in handling a family case." Her words sounded reasonable and Shuai decided to make an investigation. Then he found the young man's mother had two daughters-in-law. The elder son was a merchant doing business away from home and her younger son stayed at home and controlled family affairs. Her elder son's wife was eloquent and malicious; the younger son's wife was not good with words but kind-hearted.

Magistrate Shuai arrived at the young man's home, where he found that the elder son's wife was crying without tears while the younger son's wife was weeping sadly. The magistrate then began to question them. The elder son's wife said: "Yesterday my sister-in-law served our mother not fish meat but the leftover bits. No wonder she got into a rage and drowned herself."

But the younger son's wife said: "After I cooked some fish yesterday, I chose one of the bigger fish, picked out its bones, and brought it to our mother. I don't know why she thought it was the leftovers and then left in a rage."

Magistrate Shuai made an investigation among neighbors and discovered some inconsistencies in the story of the elder sister. He interrogated the elder son's wife again and she admitted under threat that when she smelt fish that day, she went to the kitchen and saw her sister-in-law picking off fish bones with care. She was very jealous of her and went to their mother-in-law telling the old lady that her sister-in-law was going to serve her with fish dregs.

Magistrate Shuai then wondered why the younger son so mistrusted his own wife as to sue her. Then he had the elder son's wife interrogated once more and she was intimidated into telling the whole truth. It turned out that this woman and the youngest son were having an affair and she was conniving with him to get rid of his wife.

When Magistrate Shuai was about to announce the court verdict, he heard his wife was signaling him to withdraw behind the screen. He retired from the courtroom and discussed the case with his wife. His wife advised him not to announce the verdict until he found out whether the old lady was really dead or not. Just at that moment *yamen* runners reported that the old lady arrived with her elder son requesting a hearing. The old lady said that as she was crying by the riverside, her elder son's boat arrived at the shore. After having learned why his mother was so upset, the elder son said to his mother: "Taking off the fish bones for you is a filial behavior. It shows that the sister-in-law respects you. You wronged her." The old lady felt ashamed.

Magistrate Shuai then decided: the elder son's wife and the younger son were to be punished and the old lady could learn a lesson from it; the elder son was to be praised and the younger son's wife was to be cited for her good deeds.

The news spread far and wide. Folks said admiringly, "Even an upright official finds it hard to settle a family quarrel, nevertheless Shuai, the Blue Sky, has the case well handled."

This story thus gave rise to the saying "Even an upright official finds it hard to settle a family quarrel." People use it to describe the complexity of problems within one's family.

路遥知马力，日久见人心

lù yáo zhī mǎ lì,　　rì jiǔ jiàn rén xīn

DISTANCE TESTS
A HORSE'S STAMINA;
TIME REVEALS A MAN'S HEART

路遥和马力本是结拜兄弟。路遥是大哥，已有妻室，马力是小弟，尚未完婚。路遥家境贫寒，马力却是豪门子弟。因此路遥经常得到马力的接济。

　　一天，路遥对马力说想出外谋生，希望马力帮他照顾妻子，马力让他放心。

　　次日清晨，马力送别路遥后，派一家丁，套了三辆马车，满载日常用品，送到路遥家中。此后，每隔十天半月，马力就派人去路家问候，并带些东西给路妻，路妻想："这倒不错，比丈夫在家时生活还有保障，不用干活就能丰衣足食。"心里感谢丈夫交的好朋友。

　　半年之后，情况有所变化，马力家丁不再到路家送东西了。一两个月过去了，路妻开始变卖马力送来的物品度日。不到半年，屋内的东西都卖光了。她开始寻求生活的出路。由于她从小学了一手好针线活，就每天纳鞋底做布鞋。不知是因为路妻的手艺好，还是因为大家同情她，无论她的鞋卖多高的价钱，总是被一抢而光。

　　转眼过了十多年。在一个风雪之夜，路遥回来了。当他得知自他走后，马力从未来看过他的妻子，半年以后也不送东西来了，不禁叹息："人在人情在，人走一场空啊！"

　　路遥回家的消息很快传开。第二天，马力派人来请路遥赴宴接风洗尘，路遥闭门不见。马力亲自登门相请，跪在门前，路遥才勉强进了马府。席间，路遥质问马力为何不照顾嫂嫂。马力见此情景，把路遥领到后花园，打开一间大屋子，请路遥进屋观看。路遥刚迈进门坎，顿时目瞪口呆，只见屋里堆满了一双双布鞋，他顿时明白了，羞愧地退出门外，跪在马力面前。

　　马力急忙扶起路遥说道："大哥临行的嘱托，小弟我一刻也没有忘记过，日夜盼着你归来，不想你一去就是十年。我本想资助嫂嫂丰衣足食，又怕嫂嫂一旦因生活宽裕，游手好闲，惹是生非，我怎对得起哥哥。可敬嫂嫂心灵手巧能自行谋生，正合我意，我便派人将她每次卖剩的鞋统统买了。"

　　路遥听后，凝视马力良久，半晌才说出一句话来："路遥知马

132

力,日久见人心。"

　　后来,"路遥知马力,日久见人心"这句俗语就流传开了,形容与人相处日子久了,才能看出他真正的品质。

Lu Yao and Ma Li were sworn brothers. Lu Yao, the elder brother, was poor and had a wife to support. Ma Li, the younger brother, was from a rich family and single. Considering their respective positions, Ma Li often gave financial assistance to Lu Yao.

One day Lu Yao went to see Ma Li and told him of his new plans: "I am leaving to seek a job. Could you please take care of my wife?"

"Of course, you may rest assured," Ma Li answered.

The following morning, Ma Li went to see Lu Yao off. Then he sent a man to deliver three carriages of everyday household goods to Lu Yao's wife. From then on, Ma Li had things sent to Lu Yao's wife every 10 days. Lu's wife thought to herself: "I am living a better life than before. Now I have enough to eat and wear without working."

After about six months the situation changed. Ma Li stopped sending things to Lu Yao's wife. A couple months later, Lu Yao's wife was forced to sell the things Ma Li had given her. Within half a year, all the things in the house were sold. She had to find a way to make a living by herself. Fortunately, she was good at needlework and so she made cloth shoes and sold them at the market. She didn't know whether it was because of the quality of the goods or the sympathy of the customers, but all her shoes were immediately sold no matter how high the price.

More than 10 years elapsed. One night when it was snowing, Lu Yao came back home. Upon learning that Ma Li had never paid a visit to his wife and stopped giving her financial help half a year after he left home, he sighed: "Friendship cools as friends separate."

The news that Lu Yao had come home was soon known by everyone. The following day, Ma Li sent a man to invite Lu Yao to a welcoming banquet. Lu Yao closed the door and refused the invitation. Ma Li came to invite him in person, kneeling in front of his door. Lu Yao went to the banquet reluctantly. During the dinner, Lu Yao asked Ma Li why he had neglected his wife during the years. Ma Li stood up and took Lu Yao to the rear garden, where he opened a big storeroom full of cloth shoes. At the sight of these shoes, Lu Yao was dumbstruck. He understood everything. Ashamed, he immediately kowtowed to Ma Li.

Ma Li hurried to help Lu Yao up, saying: "I never forgot to take care of my sister-in-law all these years. Moreover, I eagerly anticipated your return every day. You were gone for such a long time. In the beginning I sent your wife enough to eat and wear, but I was afraid that once she became rich, she would take it all for granted and aspire to a different life that did not include you. If I had allowed this to happen I would not be able to face you. Fortunately, your wife is good at sewing and can make a living by herself. This is a much more positive situation. I sent my men to the market to buy all the shoes she could not sell each time."

Lu Yao stared at Ma Li for a long time, then he said: "Distance tests a horse's stamina; Time reveals a man's heart."

Later Lu Yao's words became a saying. Today it is used to mean that a person's true character is revealed only after one has gotten to know the person for a long time.

跳 进 黄 河 洗 不 清

tiào jìn huáng hé xǐ bù qīng

SOMETIMES ONE CANNOT CLEAR ONESELF EVEN IF ONE JUMPS INTO THE YELLOW RIVER

据说黄河的水在很早以前，清澈见底。后来是怎么变黄的呢？这里还有一个耐人寻味的故事。

从前，在黄河岸边的一个小小的村子里，住着一个姓黄的年轻人，从小没念过书，因为他排行第三，人们都叫他黄三。他种田、捕鱼，样样都行，还有一手石匠手艺。他二十岁时娶了妻子，生活和谐、美满。

到了冬天农闲季节，黄三又像往年一样，外出干点石匠活，挣几个钱补贴家用。临行前对他妻子说，少则一个月，多则四十天，年前一定赶回来。

黄三走后，黄妻一个人在家，天天数着日子，盼望丈夫早些回来。谁知到了腊月，黄三连音信都没有，黄妻有些着急，每天几次到大路口去等丈夫。

这一天，天刚黑，黄妻远远地看见一个挑担子的人朝村口走来，她急忙迎上前去，谁知待来人走近一看，却是一个三十多岁的陌生人。黄妻扫兴地正准备往回走，忽然被来人叫住，向她打听黄三的住处。来人一听说黄三在外做工还没回来，便自称是黄三的老朋友，且有黄三的口信捎来。黄妻连忙热情地将客人请进家里，又是烧水，又是做饭。陌生人告诉黄妻，黄三手上的活还没完，过几天一定回来，劝黄妻不要着急。

吃完饭，天已经黑了，外面飘起了鹅毛大雪，来人急着告辞上路。黄妻有心留他住下，但留宿一个男人，怕别人说闲话，又一想，既是丈夫的朋友，这冰天雪地，黑灯瞎火，让他到哪里去安身呢？于是便收拾一间空房，让来人住下了。第二天一大早，客人便上了大路。

其实这位来送信的陌生人，原也不是什么坏人，早先也确实和黄三在一起干过石匠活，知道黄三住在这里。这年因急着赶回家过年，天黑时，路过这个小村庄，忽然想起黄三。听说黄三还没回来，便编造假话，混碗饭吃。没想到这件小事却给黄妻带来杀身之祸。

就在陌生人走后没几天，黄三果真赶回家来。黄妻高兴得问长问短，又提起了前几天来人捎信的事。本来还满脸笑容的黄三，听着听着，不觉皱起眉头，一连串问了三嫂许多关于那人的问题，并说不记得托人捎信的事。黄妻觉得委屈、冤枉，眼泪不住地流下来。黄三虽心里怀疑，嘴上却说："不知道就算了吧！别哭了。"

虽然两人没再说什么，可这一夜却各怀心事。

第二天，黄妻和往常一样忙着做家务。平日，村里人见到黄妻总是有说有笑，可今天好像谁都不愿和她多说一句话，有人竟远远地躲着她。她为丈夫做了可口的饭菜，可黄三只吃了几口，便借口有事出门走了。直到深夜，才见黄三喝得醉醺醺地回来了。进门一句话也没说，便倒在炕上睡着了。

三更过去了，窗外夜色里，不时传来河水的咆哮声。可怜的黄妻悄悄地推开了房门，一步步走向河边。她没有哭泣，也没有呼喊，只是用她那双善良的，却已经红肿了的双眼，回头望了望黑暗中的家门，然后两眼一闭，纵身跳进了汹涌冰冷的河水里。只是那河水顿时掀起了巨大的浪涛，狂怒地拍击着河岸，似乎在为屈死的三嫂鸣诉着不平。

第二天，人们发现在河的中央，出现了一座巨大的黄土丘，人们都说那就是黄妻变的。河水不停地冲刷着，从那以后，清清的河水就变得浑黄起来。黄三嫂本想以一死表明自己的清白，谁料到反使清清的河水变为浑黄。因而，后来每当人们遇到冤屈而又说不清楚的事，总要说上一句："跳进黄河也洗不清。"

后来，"跳进黄河洗不清"这句俗话就在民间流传开了。

It is said that the water of the Yellow River was originally clear. Why has it turned yellow? There is a story behind it.

In ancient times there was a young man named Huang San who lived in a small village by the Yellow River. He was good at farming and fishing and was also a well-known stonemason in that area. At 20, he married a girl and led a harmonious and happy life.

Winter was the slack season for farming. As usual, Huang San had to do masonry jobs in other villages to earn some extra money. Upon departure, he told his wife that he would return home in 30 or 40 days. Anyway, he assured his wife, he would definitely return before the Spring Festival.

After her husband left, the wife eagerly counted the days and hoped her husband would come back early. Soon it was December and nobody heard anything from the mason. Deeply worried, the wife went to the roadside expecting her husband's return several times a day.

One day, as it was turning dark, she saw a man carrying a pole on his shoulder coming toward the village. She hurried forward to meet him but as the man came close, she saw a stranger in his thirties. When she was about to turn back the man asked her where Huang San's home was. The wife answered that he was not at home. The stranger said that he had a message from Huang San. Then the wife warmly invited the guest home and served him with hot drinks and food. The guest told Huang's wife that Huang had not yet finished his work and would come back soon.

By the time they had finished dinner it was already dark and snowing heavily. The guest stood up and bid his kind host farewell. Huang's wife did not know what to do. On the one hand, she did not want to send the man into the cold night, and on the other hand, she was afraid there might be gossip about her having a man in her house. But as he was a friend of her husband's and had no other place to find a shelter, after long deliberation she decided to prepare a room and have the guest stay over night. Early next morning, the guest went away.

As a matter of fact, the guest was not a bad man. He really had worked as a mason with Huang some time ago and knew that Huang lived in this village. He was hurrying back home for the new year and didn't stop in a town where he could find a place to sleep over night. When he went through Huang's village, it was already dark. He suddenly thought of Huang. He told a fib to Huang's wife that he was delivering a message from Huang in order to find a shelter. But he didn't expect this could have brought dire consequences to Huang's wife.

A few days after the stranger left, Huang returned. His wife was happy to see him back and asked him about life in other villages. But when she mentioned the man who sent a message for her, Huang's smile was replaced by a puzzled look on his face. As he listened, his brows were knitted in consternation. He asked many questions about the messenger and finally said that he had not asked that man to send any message. His wife felt wronged and broke into tears. Huang listened his wife's story with suspicion but consoled her with: "Don't take it too seriously, no need for any more tears."

Although they did not exchange any more words that evening, each of them had different thoughts and worries.

The next day, Huang's wife was busy with household chores as usual. Ordinarily, villagers would exchange greetings and share jokes with her, but today it seemed that nobody would talk to her, and some people even began to avoid her.

Huang only ate a little of the delicious food she cooked for him and went out. When he finally came home at midnight, he staggered in, reeking of alcohol. Without a word, he dropped on the bed and went to sleep.

The river roared through the cold night. Huang's wife quietly pushed open the door of the house and walked to the riverside shivering in the cold. She looked back once more at her house shaded by darkness, her eyes swelling with tears, then she threw herself into the turbulent and icy cold waves. The river tide suddenly rose, angrily crashing the bank, as if grieving over the fate of Huang's wife.

The next day, a large mound of yellow soil appeared in the middle of the river. It was said that the mound was the reincarnation of Huang's wife. With the river's continuous flow, the clear water from up-stream began to turn muddy and yellow. Huang's wife had thought that her death would prove her innocence but did not expect that the clear river water would turn muddy because of it. Since then, whenever people come across a case in which they are hopelessly misunderstood and wronged they would say, "Sometimes one can't clear oneself even if one jumps into the Yellow River."

This remark has become a saying and it has been commonly used among people over years.

三百六十行 行行出状元

sān bǎi liù shí háng háng háng chū zhuàng yuán

IN ANY PROFESSION THERE IS SOME ONE WHO EXCELS ALL THE REST

宋朝时，有一个名叫叶元清的人考中了状元。按照宋朝的惯例，凡是新科状元都要骑上高头大马，在都城跑上一圈，以示威风。叶元清当然也不例外。

这天，叶元清坐在马上，前呼后拥，得意洋洋地在街上走着。来到一个十字路口时，有一个樵夫竟不回避，照直往前走。衙役们高喊让道，樵夫非但不让，反而停在路口，大声说道："新科状元有什么了不起，不就是会舞文弄墨吗？要不是我小时候家里穷，也能弄个状元当当呢！"

叶元清听了此话，心中不觉大怒，他吩咐随从们站住，自己上前指着樵夫的鼻子说："你还想当状元，真是不自量力！还是老老实实砍你的柴吧！"

樵夫听了不以为然，反而说道："世上的学问多得很，就说砍柴吧，我想怎么砍就怎么砍，你行吗？"

状元不服气，令衙役去找了块方木，又叫木匠弹上线，然后让樵夫把方木沿线劈开。樵夫看了看，举起斧头往下一劈，正巧劈在线上。旁边的人看了十分佩服。

这时，一个老翁挤了进来，嚷着说："这有什么了不起，可惜我是卖油的，不是樵夫，要不然我也能这样。"

叶元清见又来了一个奇人，于是说道："我买你二两油，但不许用秤称，而是用手倒。"

卖油翁从口袋里拿出一个小瓶，又在瓶口上放了个铜板，最后，右手拿起油桶往下倒油，只见那油如同线一样落入瓶中。拿起铜板一看，上面没沾一点油，再拿起小瓶一称，不多不少，正是二两。四周的人都惊呆了。

叶元清看了两人的表演，感慨地说："三十六行，行行出状元，我这个新科状元没什么好骄傲的。"于是打转马头就回去了。

后来，人们把三十六行改为三百六十行。俗语"三百六十行，行行出状元"就流传下来，用来说明只要有才能，不论做什么工作都能出成绩。

During the Song Dynasty (960-1279), there was a man named Ye Yuanqing who came first in the highest imperial examination. According to custom, all who came first in the examinations were conferred the title of *zhuangyuan** and would tour the capital city on horseback to be admired by people all over the city. Ye was no exception.

On that day, trotting down the street on a fine horse and accompanied by a group of servants, Ye was full of pride and complacence. The procession arrived at a street crossing where a woodcutter was in the way. He made no effort to move. The servants shouted: "Make way! Make way!" The woodcutter retorted loudly: "What's so extraordinary about a new *zhuangyuan*? All he can do is playing with words. Isn't that true? If my family was not poor when I was young, I could acquire the title of *zhuangyuan* also."

In a rage, Ye dismounted from horseback to face the woodcutter himself. Pointing his finger at the woodcutter's face, he said: "You are ridiculous! How could you compare yourself with a *zhuangyuan*! Go away and cut your wood!"

The woodcutter was not intimidated at all. He replied: "The world is full of all different kinds of knowledge. Take woodcutting for example, I can cut wood any way I like. Can you?"

The *zhuangyuan* had his servant fetch a piece of square wood with a line drawn along the center. He then challenged the woodcutter to cleave it in two precisely on the line. The woodcutter did this in a single swing of his axe. All the onlookers applauded.

At that moment an old man elbowed his way through the crowd, announced loudly: "This is nothing. I sell oil but if I were

---

*Zhuangyuan: Number One Scholar, title conferred on the one who came first in the highest imperial examination.

a woodcutter, I would be able to do this too."

Hearing this, Ye thought, "Here's another unusual person." Then he said: "I like to buy two *liang** of oil from you, but you are not to use a weight to measure it. Just pour it out for me!"

The old man took out a small bottle from his pocket and put on top of the bottle mouth a bronze coin (old Chinese money with a hole in the center). He raised his oil bucket and began to pour oil into the bottle. The oil trickled out like a thread and went directly into the bottle through the hole of the coin. When he finished someone picked up the coin and found not a single drop of oil on it. The bottle was then weighed, and the amount of oil was exactly two *liang*. Everyone was astounded at the show.

After witnessing these masterful performances, Ye sighed and said to himself: "In any profession there is someone who excell all the rest. As a new *zhuangyuan*, I shouldn't be so proud of myself." He got back on his horse and went silently back home.

This story thus gave rise to the saying which is nowadays used to mean that every trade has its master.

---

*Liang: a unit of weight (= 50 grams).

初 生 牛 犊 不 怕 虎
chū shēng niú dú bú pà hǔ

A NEWBORN CALF IS NOT
AFRAID OF A TIGER

从前在一个山村中有个农民，他养了许多头牛，每天大清早就到山坡上去放牛。其中有一头身强力壮，又很勇敢的小牛，每天放牧时只吃一会儿草，就偷偷向山坡后走去，直到晚上才回来。这件事被农民发现了。

　　一天，小牛吃了点草以后，又偷偷地向山后走去。放牛的农民就跟在后面想看个究竟。跟了半里多路，看到小牛在一个杂草丛生的山洞旁停了下来。洞中冷气森森，令人毛骨悚然。突然小牛似乎受到什么惊吓，发出一连串叫声，吓得农民浑身打颤，连忙躲到一块大石头后面。霎时，洞中蹿出一只斑斓猛虎，长啸一声向小牛扑来。小牛也不示弱，用足力气向猛虎冲去，打得满地尘土飞扬。它们直打得气喘吁吁才停下来，彼此对视着。过了一会起来又打，打了几十个回合都不分胜负。天色晚了，老虎回洞，小牛回家，农民也悄悄地跟着回来了。

　　农民想了一个办法：把小牛的两只角上绑好两把尖刀。早晨放牛，小牛又去了，它还像以往一样，把老虎引了出来。老虎出来后，它们又格斗起来。三个回合后，老虎把小牛打倒。小牛发出"哞，哞……"几声大叫，站起来，四蹄用足力气向猛虎冲了上去，猛虎躲闪不及，惨叫了一声，倒在血泊中。

　　后来"初生牛犊不怕虎"这句俗语就流传开了。人们用它形容年轻人不怕困难，不惧权威，敢作敢为。

Once upon a time, there was a peasant in a mountain village who kept a large herd of cattle. Every morning he would take his cattle to graze on the mountain slopes. One day, the peasant discovered a strong and daring newborn calf that would graze with the herd for a while and then sneak to the backside of the hill, and that it would't come back to the herd until the evening.

One day, the calf, as usual, began to quietly move to the back of the hill. Curious about the calf's movements, the peasant followed it at a little distance, until the calf stopped at the entrance of a mountain cave which was half covered by bushes and weeds. The inside of the cave was dark. As the peasant approached it, cold shivers went down his spine.

Suddenly the calf mooed continuously, expressing its fear as well. The farmer had hardly hidden himself behind a large rock when he saw a tiger leapt out from the ghastly cave. With a long howl, the beast sprang onto the calf. The calf, showing no trace of fear, dashed toward the tiger. The two fought with each other, scattering stones and dust all over the place. They matched each other so closely that after many rounds they both stopped and stared at each other vigilantly, both trying to regain their strength. Then they were ready for another battle. The fight continued in this way until it was dark and ended in a tie. The tiger retreated into the cave and the calf went back to his herd. The farmer quietly followed the young fighter back home.

Then the farmer had an idea. He tied two sharp swords onto the calf's horns.

The next morning, the calf went to face the tiger again. As before, the tiger answered the challenge when the calf came to the cave. In the third round, the calf fell at the tiger's thrust. Not giving in, it mooed loudly with anger, staggered to its hooves, and charged toward its foe. The tiger was caught unprepared and the blades on the calf's horns jabbed into the tiger's body.

The tiger let out a long howl and fell onto the ground soaked in blood.

The saying, "a newborn calf is not afraid of a tiger," was derived from this story. It is used to describe the daring spirit of young people who are not afraid of hardships and stand up to authority.

师父领进门，学艺在个人

shī fù lǐng jìn mén　xué yì zài gè rén

THE MASTER TEACHES THE TRADE, BUT THE APPRENTICE'S SKILL IS SELF – MADE

春秋战国时，鲁班盖宫殿，修白塔，干的尽是鬼斧神工的活儿。天下称颂，人人敬慕。跟他学艺的人很多，他姐姐的儿子张通就是其中的一个。

张通年龄虽不大，可是肯动脑筋，加上聪明伶俐，各种活计一看就会，比别人做的活儿好，手艺也学得快。

一天，张通和鲁班在院里做木狗。两人做的木狗的模样和毛色一模一样，可做完后，鲁班的木狗又蹦又跳，叫个不停；张通做的狗却只会跑不会叫。张通问舅舅是什么原因，舅舅却笑而不答。张通只好去求舅母帮忙。

鲁班回家后，妻子问他为何张通做的狗不会叫。鲁班知道她是代外甥来探听，十分生气，他说："你们女人嘴大舌头长，打听这做什么？"说完气冲冲地走了。

天亮后，张通来找舅母，询问结果。舅母把鲁班的话说了一遍。张通一听，一下子明白了，忙转身取下木狗的头修理。说也奇怪，修理了狗头和嘴巴，木狗马上乱叫乱跑起来。

鲁班回来后，见张通做的木狗也会叫了，十分惊奇。他想：这孩子真聪明，把我的手艺全学会了，现在只剩最后一手了。于是鲁班亲自做了一个木人和一匹木马。做好后对张通说："你的手艺已学成，该去串四方，为天下人做事啦！"张通含泪跨上木马。可木马怎么打也不走，鲁班对准马尾巴下敲了两斧子，木马立即腾空而起。他又朝木头人头上敲了两下，木头人挑着工具担子，也飞快地赶了上去。

回家不久，张通也做出了木人、木马。他又刻苦钻研，制造出更高明的运输工具—木牛。这种木牛不光会走山路，还能驮两三百斤重物呢！

原来，在鲁班做木人、木马的时候，张通已暗暗把图样记在心里。他骑上木马后，木马不动，鲁班叫他朝前看，他却留神后面，听出了鲁班敲斧头的部位，偷偷学会了舅舅的全部手艺。

后来，人们从这个故事引申出了"师父领进门，学艺在个人"这句俗语，用来说明老师的作用是启发、引导，要想学好一门技术，还要靠学生自己勤于动脑、努力钻研。

Lu Ban, a master craftsman in the Spring and Autumn Period (770-221), is commonly regarded as the God of Carpentry. All his works including palaces and pagodas are examples of superlative craftsmanship. Many people came to learn from him and be his apprentices. Zhang Tong, son of Lu Ban's sister, was among them.

Though young in age, Zhang Tong was smart, quick and able to complete a new job after he took only one look at the pattern. He learned everything faster than anyone else and excelled in every job he was given.

One day, Zhang Tong and Lu Ban were both making wooden dogs. The two wooden dogs looked exactly the same, in shape, skin and hair. However Lu's dog was able to jump and bark, while Zhang's dog could neither move nor bark. Zhang asked his uncle why but the master answered only with a smile. Zhang went to ask his aunt, Lu's wife, for help.

When Lu returned home, his wife asked him why Zhang's dog did not bark. Realizing that she was trying to help her nephew, Lu turned on her angrily: "You women have a loose tongue and a big mouth. What do you want to know about this for?" Without another word, he turned and left.

The next day, Zhang came to see his aunt again, hoping for an answer. His aunt repeated what Lu had said and Zhang suddenly realized the hidden meaning of this message. Zhang immediately went to repair his dog, he fixed the wooden dog so that it could bark and run as Lu's dog could.

Seeing Zhang's dog barking, Lu was surprised. He admired Zhang's intelligence and said to himself that this boy was so clever that he had learned all the skills but one. So Lu made a wooden man and a wooden horse and told Zhang Tong: "You have completed your apprenticeship successfully and it is time for you to travel to different places and apply your skills to help people." With tears in his eyes, Zhang got on to the back of the wooden horse. But the horse wouldn't move no matter how hard Zhang beat it. After Lu swung an ax and hit the horse twice under the tail, the horse flew up in the air. Then Lu hit the head of the wooden man twice. The man, carrying a full load of tools and luggage on his shoulder, swiftly caught up with the horse.

After Zhang returned home, he worked on his own wooden man and horse. Then he designed a wooden ox himself. It provided a means of transportation and was able to walk on a mountain path with a load of 200 or 300 *jin*.

When Lu Ban was making his wooden horse and wooden man, Zhang had memorized the design in his mind. He had also memorized the exact position where Lu had struck the horse behind to make it move. By paying close attention Zhang had secretly learned all of his uncle's skills.

Later on, "the master teaches the trade, but the apprentice's skill is self-made" became a saying. It is used to tell people that the master initiates the apprentice, but his skill depends on his own efforts.

远亲不如近邻

yuǎn qīn bù rú jìn lín

A NEAR NEIGHBOR IS BETTER THAN A DISTANT RELATIVE

传说古时候，蔚县（今属河北省）南乡府有个张员外，他与妻子两人为人善良，深得民心，就是有个儿子不称心。他儿子叫张清，生来好吃懒做，整天不是吃喝玩乐，就是赌博。没多久就把家里的积蓄输光了，气得张员外夫妻俩大病一场，很快就去世了。

父母过世后，张清整天呆在赌场里。没多久就穷得什么也没有了，只好走村串户靠乞讨为生。

有一年冬天，风雪交加。张清又冷又饿，就跑到舅舅家，他舅舅也是个员外，见他穿得又脏又破，就把脸一沉，让家人把他打出门外。张清被舅舅赶出来以后，又生气、又着急、又后悔，想起小时候富裕的生活，心头一酸，就哭起来。他越哭越冷，几乎冻僵了。

这时，张清的邻居张江在回来的路上看见他躺在地上，就把他背回家中，给他暖身子。张清醒过来后，张江又给他做饭；张清饭吃不下，水喝不进，张江就给他请医生看病。张清非常感动。

后来，张清病好了，人也变得勤劳了。他和张江两个人，农闲时砍柴，农忙时种地，没过几年两人的生活就富裕了。各自娶了妻，盖了房，两家住在一个院里，就像一家人似的。人们见了都说："真是远亲不如近邻呀！"

后来，"远亲不如近邻"这句俗语就传开了，说明邻里之间如果相处得好，会比疏远的亲戚关系更加亲近。

In ancient times, there was once a landlord named Zhang in Nanxiang, Weixian County (in present Hebei Province) who was kind-hearted and benevolent to the peasants. But his son Zhang Qing was a gluttonous and lazy fellow. He developed a gambling habit and eventually lost all his family's property including savings. His parents were so angry that soon both fell ill and died.

Not long after the old couple died Zhang Qing gambled away literally everything he owned, until he had to beg for a living.

One day in the winter, a snowstorm hit the area. Cold and starving, Zhang Qing went to his uncle's home seeking a sanctuary. His uncle who was also a landlord saw him shabbily dressed and bedraggled, and instead of receiving him, had him driven out.

Thinking of his happy days when he was young, Zhang Qing was full of shame and regret and broke into uncontrollable sob. Cold and heart-broken, he was almost frozen to death. At that moment, Zhang Jiang, Zhang Qing's ex-neighbor, was coming back home. Seeing Zhang Qing lying on the snow, Zhang Jiang immediately carried him back home and warmed him up. When Zhang Qing had come to his senses, Zhang Jiang cooked food for him and then had a doctor come to treat him. Zhang Qing was deeply moved.

When Zhang Qing recovered from his illness, he made a clean break with his past errors and became diligent and hard-working. He and Zhang Jiang became bosom friends. They cut wood in the slack season and did farm work in busy season. In a couple of years, the two became rich, both were married and had new houses built around the same courtyard. The two families lived a happy life together. Everybody who heard the story said: "A near neighbor is better than a distant relative."

This remark has become a commonly-used saying which means that a good neighbor is more helpful than an indifferent relative.

这 山 望 着 那 山 高
zhè shān wàng zhe nà shān gāo

IT'S ALWAYS THE OTHER
MOUNTAIN THAT LOOKS HIGHER

从前,有个姓贾的青年男子,人称贾相公。父亲去世之前,叮嘱他日后无论如何要学会一技之长,这样才能丰衣足食。于是,他辞别老母,匆匆上路,想去学艺。

一天,贾相公在路上遇见一个舞苍龙的。只见他边舞边唱:"苍龙苍龙点点头,来日吃穿不用愁;苍龙苍龙伸伸腰,金银财宝朝家抛。"贾相公正想拜他为师,却见一群顽童喊道:"来看舞苍龙的叫花子啊!"贾一听,泄了气,转身就走。

第二天,贾相公沿着江堤徘徊,听到纤夫的歌声,心中暗想:"船靠水力白赚钱,乐在舵中枕歌眠。"随即决定拜纤夫为师。当夜贾相公睡在船上,隐约听到船工在叹息:"世上若论苦,行船打铁磨豆腐。"贾相公心想,投错门儿啦,连夜就离开船上。

第三天,贾相公正走着,和一个算卦先生撞了个满怀。贾相公想:"算卦这行业不错,不用费力气就能赚到钱。"于是下决心学算卦。当然,没过几天,他又溜了。

学艺不成,贾相公垂头丧气地跑回家。老娘见了,又恨又怜,斟酌再三,想出个主意,要儿子去南山寻三十六座山峰,看哪座山上柴草茂盛,学着砍柴。于是,贾相公又穿上了布衣草鞋,从这座山到那座山,找柴草去了。找了好久,贾相公忽然又想起古人有一句话:"海深多蛟龙,山高多神仙。"一旦巧遇神仙,还愁什么金银财宝,丰衣足食呢？于是，他每站在一座山峰上眺望，总觉得远处的山要比近处的山高。这样，他爬遍了三十六座山，直到精疲力尽，瘫倒在山坡上。这时刚好从山上走下一个砍柴老汉，贾相公一见，以为是神仙下凡，便拜叩在地，求老汉收他为徒。老汉问清底细，语重心长地对他说："这山望着那山高，是任何事情也学不成的。"贾相公听罢，决定专心学一门技术。

自此，"这山望着那山高"这句俗语就流传开了。后来，人们用它形容某些人总是不满意当前的环境或工作，而羡慕别的环境或工作。

Once upon a time, there was a young man named Jia. Following the advice his father gave him on death bed, Jia said good-bye to his mother and set off on a journey to learn a trade.

Along the road he saw a man performing a dragon dance. The man was singing: "Dragon, dragon, nod your head, I will have no worries about food and dress. Dragon, dragon, stretch your waist, gold, silver and other treasure will be thrown into my house." Jia was contemplating to ask the dragon man to be his master when he heard some kids shouted: "Come on. Let's go watch the beggar and his dragon!" Jia did not want a beggar to be his master so he turned away.

The next day, he was wandering along a river when he heard a boat trackers' work song. He thought to himself: "A boat tracker makes money from the river. What fun it would be to sleep by the helm with beautiful singing in my ears." He decided to go with the boat trackers and learn from them. That night, as Jia was lying on the boat, he heard some boatmen sighing: "The greatest hardships under heaven are running a boat, forging iron and grinding bean curd." Jia became aware that he had again selected the wrong trade and left the boat right away.

On the third day, Jia met a fortune-teller. He thought: "To tell a fortune, all you need to do is talking. This must be a good trade as one can make money without hard labor." So he decided to learn fortune-telling but soon he also dropped that idea.

Having learned nothing, Jia came back home crestfallen. His mother was both angry and concerned. She thought it over and finally came up with an idea. She told her son to look over all the 36 peaks in the South Mountains, find the peak with the most trees and grass and learn to be a woodcutter. So Jia put on simple cotton clothes, straw slippers and went into the hills.

Jia walked alone in the hills for a long time. During his journey, he recalled an ancient saying: "Dragons live in deep

160

oceans and immortals live in high hills." He decided if he could find an immortal in the mountains, he would not have to worry about food, clothes or money again. With this thought in mind, he began to search for celestial beings on the top of each peak. However it seemed to him that the other peak always looked higher than the one he stood on. He covered all the 36 peaks until he was exhausted and fell down on the mountain slope. At that moment, he saw an old woodcutter walking down the slope. He thought the old man must be an immortal so he went down on his knees asking the old man to accept him as his student. But the woodcutter told the young man: "If you cannot decide what to learn you will never learn anything. Because the other peak always looks higher than the one you are standing on." Jia suddenly realized the truth of what he said and determined to learn just one skill and become successful in just one trade.

This story later gave rise to the saying, "It's always the other mountain that looks higher." Today people use it to criticize an insatiable desire. It is equivalent to the English saying, "The grass is always greener on the other side."

留得青山在 不怕没柴烧

liú dé qīng shān zài bú pà méi chái shāo

AS LONG AS THE GREEN MOUNTAINS ARE THERE, ONE NEED NOT WORRY ABOUT FIREWOOD

古时候，有个以烧木炭为业的老汉。他有两个儿子，大的叫青山，小的叫红山。老汉怕自己死了他俩争家产，就把东岗分给青山，西岗分给红山。

过了几年，老汉去世了，青山和红山按照父亲的安排，分别上了东岗和西岗。

西岗树大林密，能烧出很好的木炭。当年老汉怜惜红山年幼，所以把西岗分给了他。红山很勤劳，整天伐木烧炭，修房盖屋，日子过得挺富裕。三五年后，岗上的树木被砍光了，红山就在岗上种起了庄稼。谁知入夏以后，下了一场暴雨，雨水冲走了全部庄稼。红山只好到东岗投奔哥哥。

东岗树细林疏。青山熟悉岗上的一草一木，他先把岗上不成材的树丛砍伐下来烧炭，然后栽了很多树苗，又在岗下开荒种地，养牛牧羊。几年内虽然收入不多，由于省吃俭用，却也渡过了难关。三五年后，只见岗上树苗长大，岗下庄稼连片，更有牛羊成群。夏天下暴雨时，因东岗上有树林，雨水慢慢流到岗下，恰好灌溉了农田。这时，弟弟红山来了。

红山见哥哥这边一片兴旺景象，不免惊奇，就问青山有什么诀窍。

青山见弟弟的处境很不好，问明了缘由，感叹地说："你是吃山不养山，终究山穷水尽。我是先养山后吃山，才能山清水秀呢。"

后来，人们从这个故事中引申出"留得青山在，不怕没柴烧"这句俗语。现在多用来比喻即便一切财富都失去了，只要有好的身体，就有东山再起，重获成功的希望。

In ancient times, an old man made his living by burning charcoal. He had two sons, Qingshan (Green Hill) and Hongshan (Red Hill). Worrying that the two would fight for his inheritance after his death, the old man stipulated in his will that the eastern hill should be given to Qingshan and the western hill to Hongshan.

Years later, the old man passed away. Following their late father's arrangement, the two sons moved their respective families to the hills assigned to them.

The western hill was covered with large trees good for producing high quality charcoal; it was better land than the eastern hill. The father gave the better land to Hongshan because he was younger and less experienced. Hongshan cut wood and burned charcoal all day long. He built new houses and led a well-off life. Five years later, all the trees on western hill were cut down, and Hongshan began to plant crops over the slope. In summer, a storm hit the area and all the crops were washed away by a mountain flood. Although Hongshan was diligent, he had not planned well. He had to seek refuge with his brother.

Trees on the eastern hill were scarce and small. Familiar with all the plants on the hill, Qingshan first cut all the trees and bushes that would not grow into timber material for charcoal, then he planted many saplings and began to reclaim wasteland for crops and cattle by the foot of the hill. In the first few years, he made a modest income and the family lived a frugal life to get through the difficult time. Five years later, saplings grew up, sturdy crops formed a large carpet over the foot of the hill, and herds of cattle moved freely on the slope. A summer storm could not do any damage as the trees would hold the land together, and actually were planted to guide the rain downhill and irrigate the crops. When Hongshan came and saw this picturesque spectacle, he was very surprised and asked his brother what his secret was.

When Qingshan learned what happened to Hongshan, he could not help heave a long sigh: "You used the hill but did not know how to nurture it. It's no wonder that you exhausted all the resources on the hill. It is important to nurture your environment, which is why I now have a luxuriant piece of land."

This story gave rise to the saying, "As long as the green mountains are there, one needs not worry about firewood." Nowadays people use it metaphorically to mean that while there is life there is hope.

浪 子 回 头 金 不 换
làng zǐ huí tóu jīn bú huàn

THE RETURN OF A PRODIGAL
IS MORE PRECIOUS THAN GOLD

明朝时，有一个财主，年过半百，只有一个独生儿子名叫天宝。天宝整天游手好闲，挥金如土。老财主怕儿子这样下去保不住家业，专门请了一位先生教他读书，不准他随便出门。

天宝自幼聪明伶俐，如今被先生一管教，渐渐知书识礼。但是，几年以后，天宝的父母先后去世，天宝的学业就此中断了。天宝的先生走后，他就故态复萌，整天花天酒地，挥霍无度，不到两年，便将万贯家财花了个精光，最后落得以乞讨为生。这时天宝才后悔没听父亲的话，决心痛改前非，刻苦攻读。

在一个寒冬腊月的傍晚，天宝去外村借书归来，因地冻路滑，再加上一天没有吃东西，跌倒在路旁。这时，住在附近的王员外刚好路过，看见一个面貌清秀的乞丐，手里紧握着一本书。冻僵在路旁，不免起了怜悯之心，叫仆人把他背回家中。天宝苏醒过来之后，王员外详细询问了他的身世。后来，王员外把天宝留下了，让他教自己的女儿腊梅读书识字。从此，天宝就在王员外家勤恳地教书。

天宝开始还能专心教书，时间一长，老毛病又犯了，开始调戏腊梅。王员外知道了这件事，便写了一封信，让天宝送到苏州一孔桥边的表兄家。又给了天宝二十两银子作路费令他即日启程。

到了苏州，天宝见到了不少一孔桥，找了近半个月也没找到王员外表兄的住处。二十两银子就要花光了，在这走投无路的时候，他决定打开王员外的那封信看看。只见信上写了四句话：

当年桥下一冻丐，今日竟敢戏腊梅；

一孔桥边无表兄，花尽银钱不用回。

看完信，天宝恨不得投河自尽。可又一想：王员外救了我，我一定要挣下二十两银子还给他，当面向他请罪。想到这里，天宝振作起精神，白天帮人划船，晚上苦读诗书。三年过后，恰逢科场开考，天宝进京应试，中了举人。于是他日夜兼程，赶往家乡，去见王员外。

到了王员外家，天宝头顶二十两银子和一封信，跪在地上，口称"有罪"。王员外见跪在自己面前的举人原来是天宝，赶紧接过银子和信。他发现，信就是自己三年前写的那一封，不过信的背面添了四句话：

三年表兄未找成，恩人堂前还白银；

浪子回头金不换，衣锦还乡做贤人。

王员外又惊又喜，连忙把天宝扶起来，询问他这三年来的情况，又把腊梅许配给他。

后来，"浪子回头金不换"这句俗语就传开了，人们用它说明，从前游手好闲、不务正业的人若能痛改前非，重新做人是很令人高兴的事。

During the Ming Dynasty (1368-1644), a rich man in his fifties, had a son named Tianbao who was a spendthrift. The father was concerned that his son would squander the family's fortune and so he employed a tutor to teach his son and restricted his freedom to freely leave the house.

The precocious Tianbao soon read a lot of books and became increasingly cultured. A few years later, Tianbao's parents died and Tianbao had to stop his studies. After his tutor left, he resumed his old way of living and again led a life of dissipation. In one or two years, he squandered all his property and was reduced to begging. It was at this stage that Tianbao began to regret that he failed to follow his father's instructions and determined to mend his ways.

One winter evening, Tianbao returned from a neighboring village with borrowed books. It was cold and the road was slippery. Having nothing to eat for a whole day, Tianbao fell down on the roadside and fainted. Luckily, a local landlord named Wang went by and saw a frail-looking beggar lying unconscious on the ground with a book in hand. He was so sympathetic with the poor scholar that he had his servants carry Tianbao back to his home. When Tianbao regained consciousness, Wang inquired about his family in detail and then decided to engage Tianbao as his daughter Lamei's tutor. From then on, Tianbao taught Lamei reading and writing at Wang's home.

At the beginning, Tianbao worked diligently. However as time went on some of his past vices reappeared. Landlord Wang soon found out that he began to take liberties with Lamei. Then Wang wrote a letter and sent Tianbao to deliver it to Wang's cousin, who lived next to a One-Arch Bridge in Suzhou. For the journey's expenses, Tianbao was given 20 taels of silver and was asked to start right away. In Suzhou, Tianbao found many single-arch bridges, but it took him half a month before he was sure that Wang's cousin could not be found anywhere. Running out of money, he decided to take a look at the letter he was dispatching. It read:

> When I found you, you were only a frozen beggar under the bridge,
> And now you take liberties with my Lamei.
> Actually I have no cousin who lives by the One-Arch Bridge,
> But you don't have to return when you have spent all the money I gave you.

Tianbao felt so ashamed that he wanted to commit suicide by drowning himself in the river. But at second thought, he decided to repay Wang who had saved his life by all means and ask for his pardon. So Tianbao, plucked up his courage, worked on a boat during the day and studied at night. Three years later, Tianbao participated in an imperial examination. He succeeded and became a *juren**. With this honor, he hurried back to see Landlord Wang.

At Wang's home, Tianbao knelt down on the ground and carried a plate containing 20 taels of silver and a letter on his head. Wang recognized the man kneeling down in front of him was Tianbao. He walked up to him, took the silver and letter. It was the same letter he had written three years ago, but another four lines had been added:

> I did not find your cousin three years ago,
> Now at my benefactor's hall I pay back the money.

---

* *Juren*: The title of a successful candidate in the imperial examinations at the provincial level in the Ming and Qing Dynasties.

The return of a prodigal is more precious than gold,
I dressed up with a suit of brocade and returned an upright
man.

Surprised and overjoyed, Wang helped him up and inquired about his life for the past three years. He also promised to give Tianbao Lamei's hand in marriage.

From then on, "The return of a prodigal more precious than gold" has been used to encourage a young man who has mended his ways.

磨 刀 不 误 砍 柴 工

mó dāo bú wù kǎn chái gōng

GRINDING A CHOPPER
WILL NOT DELAY THE WORK OF
CUTTING FIREWOOD

传说，天上的七仙女嫁给凡间的董永之后，触动了六仙女的凡心。她也想悄悄离开天庭，来到人间。六仙女驾着祥云，遍游寰宇，结果在太行山麓发现了一对年轻的樵夫。她见这对年轻人长得眉清目秀，身上衣衫却十分褴褛，砍起柴来汗流浃背，不觉产生了爱怜之心，便向他俩走去。

这是一对孪生兄弟，老大叫大宝，老二叫二宝。兄弟俩每日上山砍柴，供养着老母亲。这天他俩砍好柴，正准备回家，忽见一位姑娘姗姗走来。大宝二宝只顾赶路，当他们刚刚跨进门槛的时候，六仙女也跟着进门了。

大宝十分诧异，赶紧回茅屋去请妈妈。那女子说，随爹爹逃荒至此，不料在山中遇到一只猛虎，爹爹为了保护她，竟然遭到猛虎杀害。老妈妈听后，让姑娘进屋，并让大宝二宝第二天进山去捉那老虎。六仙女说："猛虎早不知逃向何方。去哪里捉呢？只是小女举目无亲，请老妈妈作主，为我找个善良人家，做个农家媳妇，我也就满足了。"老妈妈听罢，喜不自胜，夜里悄悄问仙女可愿作她的儿媳妇，喜欢大宝还是二宝。六仙女说："您为我作主吧。"老妈妈想了好久，拿不定主意。后来，她想出了一条妙计：让兄弟俩明天都进山砍柴，谁砍得多，回来得早，就把姑娘嫁给谁。

二宝心眼多，天还没亮就起床，独自进了南山。他想，南山的柴禾嫩，一定砍得快。大宝却有意谦让弟弟，他故意将柴刀磨了又磨，太阳升到一竿高时才动身，进了北山。他想，北山上柴禾老，一定砍得慢。谁知因为他的刀快，没过多久就砍了满满一担柴禾。他又故意等到太阳落山才回到家里。不料二宝尚未回来，原来由于二宝的刀钝，直到天黑他才砍回半担柴禾，老妈妈说："你砍得这么慢，只好让姑娘嫁给你哥哥了！"六仙女笑了笑说："磨刀不误砍柴工啊！"

后来，"磨刀不误砍柴工"这句俗语就传开了。人们用它说明，要想又快又好地完成一项任务，必须进行充分的准备工作。

It is said that after the Seventh Sister of the Seven Celestial Beauties in Heaven married farmer Dong Yong, the Sixth Sister also desired to live a normal human life on the earth. Riding on an auspicious cloud, she secretly left the celestial court, traveled over the universe and finally found two twin woodcutters in the Taihang Mountains. The two brothers looked gentle and handsome but dressed in rags. They both worked very hard, soaking in sweat as they did job. The sixth sister landed on the mountain path and walked toward them.

The twins, Dabao and Erbao had to do woodcutting work to support their old mother. This day, as they tied up the wood they had cut and prepared to go home, they saw a girl approaching them. They didn't pay any attention to the girl but hurried home with their heavy load. When they entered home, Sixth Sister followed them in.

Dabao was surprised. So he went inside and asked his mother to talk to her. The girl told the family that she had fled from famine with her father and had been attacked by a fierce tiger. Her father had fought the tiger to protect her and was killed. The mother invited the girl inside and asked her sons to capture the tiger the next day. But Sixth Sister said: "The tiger must have wandered away. As I have no place to go, if you would please help me by allowing me to marry into a kind-hearted family to become a farmer's wife, I will be so grateful to you." The mother was delighted and asked the girl if she would marry one of her own sons, Dabao or Erbao. The young girl said she would like to but ask the mother to decide which one she should marry. The mother thought it over and over but could not make up her mind. Finally, she hit upon an idea. The next day she instructed her two sons to go to the hill and cut wood. The one who could cut more wood in less time would marry the beautiful girl.

Erbao was tricky and got up before dawn to go out alone. He thought to himself that trees in the southern hill had soft and tender fibers and it would take less time to cut. But Dabao, intending to let his brother win, sharpened his knife again and again and did not start off until the sun rose to the top of a long bamboo pole. He went to the northern hill as he knew that trees there were older and it would take more time to cut. But a full load of wood was collected in a little while with the sharp blade. But he delayed his return until the sun set behind the mountains. To his surprise, Erbao was still not home yet. Erbao came home when it was completely dark with only a half load because of his blunt knife. So mother announced, "Erbao, you did a slow job and the girl shall marry your brother." Then Sixth Sister smiled, remarking, "Grinding a chopper will not delay the work of cutting firewood."

Today, this saying is widely used to illustrate that more preparation may quicken the speed in doing work.

王婆卖瓜—自卖自夸

wáng pó mài guā   zì mài zì kuā

WANG PO SELLS MELONS AND PRAISES WHAT HE SELLS

宋朝时有个人，人称王婆，其实是个男人，本名叫王坡。因为他说话絮絮叨叨，做起事来婆婆妈妈，人们就送他个外号——王婆。

王婆的老家在西夏，以种瓜为生，那一带种的是胡瓜，也就是今天的哈蜜瓜。当时，宋朝边境经常发生战乱，王婆为了避难，迁到了开封府（今属河南省）乡下。他在那里把随身带来的胡瓜种栽培出来，居然保持了原来香甜的味道。第一年，王婆的胡瓜丰收，他运了一车进城去卖，可是集市上的人不认识这种古怪的瓜，端详了一番，没有一个人肯买。王婆心里着急，真想把胡瓜的妙处告诉大家，更想直起嗓子吆喝一阵。可是当时开封府商人有一条行规：只准坐卖，不准叫卖，要是违背了规矩，就得赶出集市。

王婆在集市上亏了本，只好搬到草市上去摆摊子，因为草市都是些小贩做生意的地方，商业行规管不到这里。王婆在这里卖瓜，就可以用他的三寸不烂之舌，向来往的人群夸耀他的瓜了。行人们听他把这瓜说得那么香甜，又见他把瓜切开让大家品尝。大家尝了以后，都说甜，是好瓜。一传十，十传百，王婆的瓜摊生意越来越兴隆。

一天，神宗皇帝出宫巡视，一时高兴，来到草市，只见那边挤满了人，便问左右，才知是个卖胡瓜的引来众人买瓜。皇帝一听，当即走过去观看。只见王婆正在夸耀自己的瓜好。王婆见神宗皇帝驾到，一边选了个好瓜，双手奉上，一边把这瓜的妙处又夸了一通。

神宗皇帝一尝，果然觉得甘甜异常，不禁大喜，连声称妙。又问："你这瓜既然这么好，为何要吆喝不停，难道还怕卖不出去吗？"王婆回道："这瓜是西夏品种，中原人不认识，原本没人敢吃，是我夸了一阵，才有了买主。"神宗听了，对驾前众官说："做买卖还是当夸则夸，像王婆卖瓜，自卖自夸，有何不好？"皇帝金口一开，顿时传遍了草市，不出半月，这句话就传遍了黄河南北，直到今天。人们用它比喻自我吹嘘一类的行为。

During the Song Dynasty, there was a man named Wang Po. Since he was as garrulous and fussy as a nitpicking old woman, people called him Auntie Wang (the Chinese character for auntie is pronounced *po*).

Wang Po was originally from West Xia (1038-1227), an ancient kingdom in northwest China. He was a melon grower. The kind of melon he planted was called *Hu* melon, known today as Hami melon, a variety of muskmelon common in northwest China. Auntie Wang had moved away from the bordering areas because of the constant war in the area. He sought refuge in the suburbs of the Song capital Kaifeng (in present Henan Province). There he planted *Hu* melon. The melons grew very well, with exactly the same fragrance and sweetness as in his home town. After a bountiful harvest, he shipped the melons to the urban areas for sale. However, nobody at the markets had seen this kind of strange-looking melon before and so nobody would buy the melons. Auntie Wang was so worried that he decided to hawk his melons. But unfortunately, the trade rule for Kaifeng's businessmen forbade hawking and anyone breaching the rule would be driven out of the market.

Auntie Wang did not make any money at the first fair. He moved to a small peddlers' market, where the trade rule would not be binding, and set up a stall there. Now Auntie Wang could publicly exaggerate about his melons to customers. The sensational and clamorous advertising of his melons attracted a lot of passers-by, who were willing to taste and appreciate his melon. The word soon got around and Auntie Wang's business boomed.

One day, Emperor Shenzong made an inspection trip outside the court and came to the peddlers' market purely on a whim. There he saw a large crowd and asked his men why. When he learned that it was a farmer selling melons from northwest China, he immediately went up to take a closer look. Auntie

Wang continued with his advertising, and selected the best melon and presented it to the emperor with both hands.

The emperor tasted the melon and he too found the fruit to be excellent. He praised the melon and asked Wang: "For such a good melon, why do you need to make such a noisy advertising? Are you worried that it won't sell well?" Auntie Wang replied: "The melon comes from the West Xia, people here are not familiar with it. Nobody would taste it if I did not blow my own trumpet. It is my advertising that has brought buyers here."

The emperor told the ministers at his side: "Businessmen ought to advertise what they sell. Wang Po sells melons and advertise what he sells. Isn't it appropriate?"

With the emperor's word, the saying was soon widely used to indicate self-promoting and glorifying conduct.

打 破 砂 锅 问 到 底

dǎ pò shā guō wèn dào dǐ

GETTING TO THE BOTTOM OF THE MATTER OVER A BROKEN POT

从前，在太行山下的一个小镇上，住着一户做生意的人家。婆婆办事非常认真，而儿媳却大大咧咧，因此婆媳二人常常为一些鸡毛蒜皮的小事闹得不可开交。

　　有一年春节过后，公公要到河南做生意，临行前叮嘱婆媳二人不要吵闹，若有不好解决的问题，可以写信让他回来处理。

　　公公走了半个月之后，儿媳在烧饭时把一个旧砂锅打破了。她怕婆婆责骂，就偷偷地把砂锅扔了。过了两天，婆婆发现家中少了一只砂锅，便对着儿媳大吵大骂。儿媳不得不如实说明，婆婆又让她把碎砂锅找来。碎片找来后，婆婆又提出一连串的问题。媳妇被盘问得哭笑不得，婆婆非要弄个水落石出不可，当即给远在河南的丈夫写信，要他火速回来。

　　丈夫接到急信，看过之后，知道老妻在钻牛角尖了，便及时回了信，信上写道：

　　打破砂锅问到底，

　　切莫吹毛又求疵；

　　二十年的媳妇二十年的婆，

　　互敬互重万事皆如意。

　　儿媳看见公公的来信，觉得这次纠纷是自己的责任，所以先向婆婆道歉。婆婆觉得自己小题大作，闹得家中不得安宁，错在自己这边。两人终于和好了。

　　后来，"打破砂锅问到底"这句俗语就流传下来了，人们用它形容一味追究事情的根源，非要问个水落石出不可。

A long time ago a merchant family lived in a small town at the foot of the Taihang Mountain. The merchant's wife was a very conscientious woman but her daughter-in-law was a careless sort of person. The two women always bickered with each other over trifles.

The merchant was going to Henan to do business after the Spring Festival. Before departure, he told his wife and daughter-in-law not to argue over small matters during his absence. "In case there is a real dispute that can't be solved between you, write to me and I'll come back to settle the issue," he said.

Half a month elapsed after the merchant departed from the house. One day the young woman broke an earthen pot into pieces when she was cooking a meal. Afraid that her mother-in-law would rebuke her, she threw away the shattered pot. Two days later her mother-in-law discovered that an earthen pot was missing. She raised hell and made a great fuss. Then the young woman told her what had happened. The mother asked the daughter-in-law to bring the broken pot to her. She insisted that she must find out the root of the matter and wrote to her husband to come back immediately to settle the matter.

The merchant read the letter, from which he learned his wife was bickering over an insignificant matter and had landed herself in an awkward position. He wrote back immediately, saying, "Why insist on getting to the bottom of the matter over a broken pot? This nitpicking fuss must be stopped by all means! Since you have been mother and daughter for twenty years, try to respect each other so that everything will turn out well."

The two in-laws read the merchant's letter and became aware that they both had some responsibility in the squabble. The daughter apologized to the mother and the mother in turn apologized about her nitpicking. The two ended their squabble and were reconciled.

"Getting to the bottom of the matter over a broken pot" subsequently became a saying to criticize people asking too many questions about some insignificant matter.

竹 篮 子 打 水 —— 一 场 空

zhú lán zi dǎ shuǐ   yì chǎng kōng

DRAWING WATER
WITH A BAMBOO BASKET
— NOTHING GAINED

从前,有一个叫胡元的人,一心想修炼成仙。一天,他带了干粮去寻仙拜师,历尽千辛万苦,一个仙人也没遇到,心里十分懊恼,眼看带的干粮和钱快耗尽了,只好返回家乡。

这事被八仙中的蓝采和知道了,便驾着祥云来到胡元家对他说:"如果你真心想成仙,就把我这花竹篮拿去,每天三次到河里去打水。"

胡元想,这竹篮子能打水吗?又一想仙人给的竹篮子不会错的。他一下又一下地在河里打水,篮子里的水居然一次比一次多起来。日复一日,他就这样一直打了整整十年,篮子里的水眼看就要满了,心中不免欣喜万分。

一次,胡元又到河边去打水,见一个小孩正在水里挣扎,连喊"救命",眼看就要沉下去了。胡元却视而不见,只顾打水。就在他打好水刚要离岸时,突然觉得手中一轻,竹篮里的水全都漏光了。他不由得一惊,忽然仙人蓝采和出现在他面前,对他说:"你看见孩子快要淹死了,却不去救他,可见你没有善心,既然没有善心,哪谈得上成仙?你还是在家好好种地吧!"胡元听了,非常后悔,白白打了十年水。

原来,河里的小孩是蓝采和变的。 后来,人们从这个故事中引申出"竹篮子打水 —— 一场空"这句俗语,形容一个人对某事抱了很大希望,付出了很多努力,可是最终却什么也没有得到。

A long time ago there was a man named Hu Yuan who was obsessed to become an immortal. He decided to embark on a trip to seek for an immortal. He went through many difficulties but never came across any immortals. Finally he had to abandon his mission and return home.

Lan Caihe, one of the Eight Immortals, heard something about Hu Yuan. Riding on cloud, he visited Hu Yuan at his home. He told Hu Yuan: "If you really want to become an immortal, take my bamboo basket and go to the river to draw water three times a day."

Hu Yuan thought: How can a bamboo basket draw water? But since Lan Caihe is an immortal perhaps it could be done. He tried to draw water in the river and was surprised to find the basket could keep a little water every time he drew. So he kept on drawing water with the basket for almost 10 years. The basket seemed almost full with water. Hu Yuan felt very happy.

One day Hu Yuan went to the river again to draw water. He saw a child was struggling in the river, shouting: "Help! Help!" But he didn't drop his basket in order to save the child. Instead he went on with his work. When he lifted up his heavy basket filled with water, he suddenly found the basket very light again. The water had leaked out. He was shocked. At that moment, Lan Caihe suddenly appeared before him and said: "You saw the child was going to drown, but you didn't even try to save his life. You don't have a benevolent heart. How can you become an immortal! You'd better go home and be a good farmer."

Actually the child was Lan Caihe in disguise.

"Drawing water with a bamboo basket — nothing gained" has become a popular saying. It is used to describe a man, who has placed great hopes on achieving a goal and made all efforts for it, finally find that his hard work proved to be in vain.

刘备摔孩子 — 收买人心

liú bèi shuāi hái zi shōu mǎi rén xīn

LIU BEI THROWS HIS CHILD
ON THE GROUND TO WIN OVER
THE HEART OF HIS FOLLOWERS

曹操率兵攻打樊城，刘备率领众百姓逃往江陵，命令张飞断后，赵云保护刘备的夫人和儿子阿斗。其余将士照管百姓，每天只走十多里就停下休息。

　　在景山附近，刘备的队伍被曹操的铁骑赶上，一阵混战，赵云一马当先，杀至天明，才发现夫人和阿斗不见了，只得又杀入重围，到处寻找，好不容易在墙下的枯井旁找到了母子二人，赵云请夫人上马，自己步行而战，夫人为不拖累赵云，投井而死。赵云将阿斗缚在怀中，继续作战，长坂坡一场血战，杀死曹营名将五十余人，当杀出重围时，已血满征袍。刘备为了抚慰赵云，把阿斗扔在地上说："为这孺子，几乎损失了我一员大将。"赵云从地上抱起阿斗，哭着说："云虽肝脑涂地，不能报也（我即使牺牲生命，也不能报答您的恩情）。"

　　后来，人们从这个故事中引申出俗语"刘备摔孩子——收买人心"，用来形容有目的地对他人施以恩惠，以便更好地利用他人。

During the Three Kingdoms Period (220-280), Cao Cao led a force to attack Fancheng. Liu Bei and the inhabitants abandoned the city and fled to Jiangling. Zhang Fei took up the rear to prevent advancing enemy troops from attacking the fleeing inhabitants. General Zhao Yuan received the order to protect Liu Bei's wife and son. The rest of the generals and officers were to look after the people. The withdrawal was slow. The people managed to march a short distance over only ten *li* (five kilometers) a day.

Liu Bei's troops were overtaken by Cao Cao's cavalry unit near Jingshan. A battle followed. Zhao Yuan fought the enemy till daybreak. He found that the wife and son of Liu Bei were missing. He fought his way into the enemy encirclement and he managed to find Madam Liu Bei and the child by a well. Zhao Yuan then asked the madam to ride on the horse. He would fight on foot to protect them. Madam Liu did not want to be a burden on Zhao Yuan. She jumped into the well and drowned herself. Zhao Yuan put the child on his chest covered underneath his armor. He continued the fight and killed over 50 generals of Cao Cao's army. At the end of the battle, his entire armor was stained by blood. In order to comfort Zhao Yuan, Liu Bei threw the child on the ground after Zhao Yuan brought his back to the camp. He justified his action by saying that he almost lost one of his best generals on account of the child. Zhao Yuan hurriedly picked up the child from the ground, saying that he couldn't pay back Liu Bei's benevolence and affection even if he gave his life, for his master's cause.

When people talk of this episode, they use the expression "Liu Bei throws the child on the ground to win over the heart of his followers" to indicate that sometimes people make a benevolent gesture to win over other's heart so as to better manipulate the other person.

张 飞 绣 花 — 粗 中 有 细

zhāng fēi xiù huā　　　　cū zhōng yǒu xì

ZHANG FEI DOES EMBROIDERY WORK — A CARELESS PERSON MAY POSSESS SOME REFINED QUALITIES

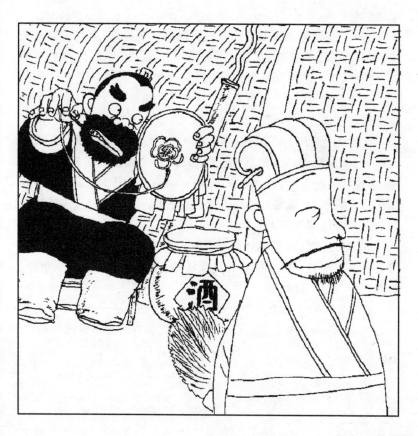

传说刘备借得荆州之后，为了扩大地盘，带着军师庞统和黄忠、魏征等率领大军去攻打四川的益州。不料在攻打雒邑的时候，军师庞统不幸中箭身亡，刘备只好写信给诸葛亮，请他入川协助指挥作战。

诸葛亮入川兵分两路，一路由自己亲自率领，另一路由张飞率领。但张飞粗心大意，诸葛亮对不太放心，便想了一个计策。他把张飞叫来，拿了一根绣花针和一根丝线，请张飞来穿针。

张飞不知道诸葛亮要做什么，心想穿就穿吧！他睁大环眼，一眨不眨地穿针，但是怎么也穿不进去。诸葛亮让张飞别急，并说一要细心，二要耐心，三要用心。三天之内把线穿进针眼，就算打了一个大胜仗。

三天之后，张飞果然把线穿进了针眼。接着，诸葛亮又交给张飞一块白绢，要他绣花，并说绣花是为了打仗。张飞这才明白，军师要他穿针、绣花的用意是告诉他打仗时要细心、谨慎。

花还没有绣，张飞就出发了。诸葛亮拨给他一万人马让他去夺取巴郡。巴郡太守名叫严颜，他和张飞只打了一仗，就被张飞活捉了。严颜拒不投降，张飞声如巨雷地吼道："给我推出去斩了！"话一出口，马上又想起绣花的事，连忙改口说道："且慢！"说着，走近严颜，亲自给他松了绑，请他坐在上座，并说刚才自己太鲁莽了。严颜见他这么谦和，忙说愿为张将军效力。结果，严颜引路，张飞带队伍顺利地到雒邑和诸葛亮会师了。

拿下雒邑之后，张飞对诸葛亮说："军师，我的花还没绣好呢！"诸葛亮满意地说："不，你的花已经绣好了！巴郡一仗打得很出色，智降严颜，粗中有细！"

后来，人们从这个故事中引申出"张飞绣花——粗中有细"这句俗语，说明有些看上去粗心大意的人，也会有细心谨慎的一面。

The legend goes that having taken over control of Jing-zhou, Liu Bei led a huge army with Pang Tong, his chief of staff, and General Huang Zhong and Wei Zheng to attack Yizhou. Pang Tong was unfortunately hit by a poisonous arrow and died during the assault on Luoyi. Liu Bei wrote to Zhuge Liang for reinforcement to continue his advance to Sichuan.

Zhuge Liang sent two columns to Sichuan, one led by himself and the other led by Zhang Fei. Zhang Fei was a rough and careless sort of fellow. Zhuge Liang conceived a plan to address the carelessness of Zhang Fei. He asked Zhang Fei to thread a needle. Not knowing what Zhuge Liang was up to, Zhang Fei tried to thread a needle with his eyes wide open. Zhuge Liang cautioned Zhang Fei to be very careful, to have patience and determination to do things. He said if Zhang Fei could manage to thread the needle in three days, he would succeed in winning a big campaign in the battlefield.

Three days later Zhang Fei succeeded in threading the needle. Again Zhuge Liang gave Zhang Fei a piece of white silk and asked Zhang Fei to embroider the silk with a design. He said that embroidery work was also for the sake of winning battles. Zhang Fei realized what Zhuge Liang wanted him to do was to be careful and exercise caution in battle.

Zhang Fei started on his march, without actually finishing his embroidery work. Zhuge Liang sent a force of 10,000 men to take Bajun. Yan Yan, the prefectural ruler of Bajun was taken prisoner by Zhang Fei after a battle. "Chop off his head right away," Zhang Fei roared. Then, he thought about how he did embroidery work. Then he changed his attitude. He untied Yan Yan, to whom he apologized for being rude. Yan Yan thought that Zhang Fei was a man of moderation. He told Zhang Fei that he would render him any service. Yan Yan led the way and Zhang Fei succeeded in joining forces with Zhuge Liang in Luoyi.

Having taken Luoyi, Zhang Fei told Zhuge Liang that he still hadn't finished his embroidery work. Zhuge Liang said satisfactorily: "You have completed your task. You have won a big battle in Bajun. You have used wisdom to make Yan Yan surrender to you. Though you are a rough sort of person but we see that you are learning to be careful in doing things."

This story thus gave rise to the saying, "Zhang Fei does embroidery work — a careless person may possess some refined qualities." Nowadays it is still commonly used among people.

兔 子 的 尾 巴 — 长 不 了
tù zi de wěi ba   cháng bù lǎo

THE TAIL OF A RABBIT
CANNOT BE LONG

传说，世上最早的一对兔子尾巴很长。不料有一回，却因为耍小聪明把漂亮的尾巴弄成了现在这个样子。

　　有一天，这对兔子在一条小河边上玩耍，看见对岸有一片嫩绿的草，很想过去饱餐一顿。但是兔子不会游水，正想不出主意，突然看见水里有一只乌龟。兔子就探头问乌龟："你的儿女很多吗？是一个大家庭吗？我们来比一比，看谁家的人多。"乌龟说："怎么比法？"兔子说："今天先数你的儿女，明天再数我们的儿女。你把你的儿女都叫来，从河这边排到河那边，我们从这边跳过去。"乌龟就把自己的儿女叫来，整整齐齐排成两行，浮在水面。兔子就来数了，他们俩一齐从乌龟们身上跳过去，一边跳，一边数，数着数着，快到对岸了，两个兔子得意极了，就使劲一跳，一边说："傻瓜，我可骗了你们了。"不料，它们得意得太早了，这一跳是跳上去了，一对尾巴却还拖在后面，在岸边的一对乌龟听见了，就一口咬住它们的尾巴，要问它们骗了什么。两只兔子一挣，逃脱了，可是尾巴却被咬断了。

　　从此，兔子尾巴就成了现在这样短短的。"兔子尾巴——长不了"便成了人们常说的一句俗语，用来形容某人得意的时候不会长久，常含贬义。

It is said that the first couple of rabbits had long tails. One day, they tried to take advantage of the tortoise. In doing so, they lost their long tails.

The story says that one day this couple of rabbits were playing by the river. They saw the meadow on the opposite bank was luxuriant and wanted to go there to eat the tender and green grass. But they were unable to swim across. They saw a tortoise in the river. So they conceived a plan to take advantage of it. They said to the tortoise: "Do you have many children? Is yours a big family? Let's have a contest to see whose family is bigger." "How do we make the contest?" the tortoise asked. "Let's count your children," replied the rabbits. "You ask your children to form two lines on the river. As we step on them to cross the river we can count how many they are." So the tortoise asked its children to form into two lines on the river. So the rabbits jumped on the back of each tortoise as they went along, they counted their number on the way. When they were approaching the bank, they got excited, and spoke out: "Stupid tortoises, we fooled you!" But as they were jumping to the opposite bank of the river, their long tails were left trailing in the water. The last tortoise who heard their remark immediately bit into the tails of the rabbits, demanding: "What's your trick?" The rabbits managed to escape with a jerk. But in doing so, they lost their long tails.

A popular saying now goes: "The tail of a rabbit cannot be long," indicating a misdeed cannot prevail for long.

茶壶里煮饺子 —— 心里有数

chá hú lǐ zhǔ jiǎo zi   xīn lǐ yǒu shù

COOKING DUMPLINGS IN A TEAPOT — HAVE A DEFINITE IDEA OF WHAT ONE IS DOING

传说东晋大书法家王羲之小时候拜卫夫人为师,学习书法。到了成年时,他已小有名气了,人们常请他书匾刻碑。从此他就骄傲起来,整日游山玩水,不再勤奋学习,刻苦练习书法了。

一天,他到河北一带游山访友。不觉天色已晚,他就到燕山下一间茅草屋里借宿,这里住着一个老婆婆。老婆婆先给他沏了一壶茶,接着就给他准备饭。她先捅旺炉火,然后往火上放了一把粗嘴的铜茶壶。老婆婆上炕和王羲之对面坐着,背着炉火和铜壶捏起饺子来。每捏一个饺子,就将右手向后轻轻一抖,连头也不回,那饺子就像长了翅膀一样,正好跌进壶嘴。王羲之看了感到十分惊奇,就对婆婆说:"这太神奇了。"老婆婆笑着说:"熟能生巧,只要做得久了,就有准儿了。我虽然没用眼睛看,但这饺子多大,壶嘴多粗,离壶多远,该用多大的劲儿,我心里都有数。不过也得常练,多日不练就扔不准了。"

王羲之从老婆婆的这番话里受到启发。吃过饭后,他谢过老婆婆,连夜动身返回山东家乡。他整理好文房四宝,访名家,拜名师,重新练习书法。后来,他的字越写越好,终于成为我国历史上有名的大书法家。从此,民间就留下了一句俗语:"茶壶里煮饺子——心里有数。"

Wang Xizhi, the famous calligrapher of the Eastern Jin Dynasty (317-420), once learned calligraphy under Madam Wei when he was a boy. When he came of age he had made a name for himself. Many people asked him to write characters to be inscribed on stone tablets or wooden boards. He became conceited and began to tour many places and enjoy himself, no longer diligently apply himself to his studies and calligraphy writing.

One day as Wang was touring and visiting friends in Hebei, he stopped and spent a night in a straw hut at the foot of Mount Yan. The inhabitant of the hut was an elderly woman, who boiled him a pot of tea. In preparation to cook a meal for him, she stirred up the fire and put a brass tea pot with a big spout on it. Then with her back facing the pot, she sat on her *kang* (a kind of earthen bed which is common in the rural areas of north China) to knead dumplings. Each time after she kneaded a dumpling she would throw it behind her back without turning her head. To Wang's surprise, all the dumplings flew exactly into the spout of the brass pot as if they were some winged creatures! "This is inconceivable!" he said. The elderly woman replied: "Practice makes perfect. If you do it often enough you are sure to hit the target. Although I didn't use my eyes but I knew how big I made the dumplings and I knew the size of the spout of the pot; I knew the distance and I knew how much force I should use to throw it into the pot. But I must practice very often. If I stop doing it for a few days, I shall not be able to make it."

Wang Xizhi was inspired by the woman's remarks. He ate the dumplings and thanked the woman for her hospitality. He went back to Shandong that evening and brought his stationeries for another tour to visit famous calligraphers and started again to study the art of calligraphy. He practiced calligraphy without respite and finally became the most famous calligrapher in Chinese history. This story later gave rise to the saying, "Cooking dumplings in a teapot — have a definite idea of what one is doing." Nowadays it is still commonly used among people.

蚊子叮菩萨 —— 认错人

wén zi dīng pú sà　　rèn cuò rén

MOSQUITO BITES BUDDHA
—— A PERSON IS MISJUDGED

很久以前的一个夏天,在一座大山的山沟里飞着一只蚊子。飞着飞着,蚊子突然觉得肚子里饿得发慌。可这荒山野地,到哪儿能找到吸血的对象?蚊子想,不管怎样,到前面看看再说。飞了好长一段路程,才发现大山下有个山洞,里面,一只苍蝇正在吃一堆臭肉。蚊子问苍蝇什么地方有人住,它要吃活人活畜的鲜血。苍蝇告诉它,前面有一座庙,庙里有一个胖子,可以去吸他的血。蚊子马上告别苍蝇,一展翅飞到那座庙里去了。

庙里大殿上有一个胖子,眼睛半睁半闭,盘腿而坐,双手合十,像是在闭目养神。蚊子悄悄地飞过去,轻轻地落在胖子的手上,用脚磨了磨嘴巴,开始了它吸血的习惯动作。奇怪的是它怎么也吸不到血,蚊子想:也许此处皮厚。但是一连换了好几个地方都是一样。

蚊子不死心,一心想吸胖子的血,它相信自己的嘴巴是锋利的。它在胖子身上呆了十几天,也没有吸到一滴血,最后,它精疲力尽,活活饿死了。

究竟是怎么回事呢?

原来,蚊子所叮的那个胖子是庙里的一尊菩萨塑像。

人们根据这个传说故事引申出了俗语"蚊子叮菩萨——认错人"。通常用来形容判断力欠佳,把品质恶劣的人看成了好人。

One summer day long before, a mosquito was flying in the mountain gully. It got hungry and couldn't find any creature to suck blood from to feed itself in the desolate mountain. At the foot of the mountain, it discovered a cave in which a fly was eating rotten meat. The mosquito asked the fly where it could find some living inhabitants from whom it could suck blood. The fly told it that there was a temple in front where there sat a fat man and that it could suck the blood of that man. The mosquito said thanks and flew to the temple.

There was a fat person in the temple. His eyes were half shut and half open, as if he was meditating. He was seated with crossed legs. The mosquito flew to the hands of the fat man. It wiped its mouth and began its habitual movements to get ready for the bite. But no matter how hard it bit, it could not suck any blood out of the person. Perhaps this part of the muscle is particularly thick, he thought. "Let me suck another place," said the mosquito to itself. But again, it failed. The mosquito kept on sucking blood from the fat man, for it believed that its mouth could surely pierce the man's skin. But no matter how hard it bit into the skin of the man it simply could not extract any blood. The mosquito was exhausted in the end and died of starvation.

The death of the mosquito was caused by its misjudgment. Of course, the fat man was only a sculpture of a Buddha.

The saying, "mosquito bites Buddha — a person is misjudged," was derived from the aforementioned story. Today people use it to mean mistaking a man of bad character for a good man.

没 良 心

méi láng xīn

WITHOUT CONSCIENCE

相传，古时候有个王木匠，各种木工活都会做，在当地名气很大，很多人都来请他做家具。邻村有个年轻人名叫张金，一心想拜王木匠为师，把他的手艺学到手。一天，张金来找王木匠谈这件事，王木匠说："你要想学我的手艺，必须答应我一个条件。我已经六十多岁了，没有儿女，以后干不了活时要靠你养老。"张金毫不犹豫地回答："您只要把手艺全部教给我，我就作您的儿子，为您养老送终。"他一边说，一边跪下给王木匠磕头。

张金拜师后，就住在王木匠家。开始，他很听话，干活勤快，对老木匠也十分尊敬。王木匠把他当成自己的儿子一般对待，将一些绝活传授给了他。不到半年，张金就能单独到外面干活了。他觉得自己能挣钱了，就变了心。一天，张金借回家探亲为理由离开了王木匠家。王木匠在家里等啊，等啊，可是一年过去了，徒弟还是没有回来。后来，他听说徒弟单独干活挣钱去了，非常伤心，他想：幸亏我没把最拿手的绝活教给他！

不久，王木匠病了，就做了一个木头人来帮自己干活。这个木头人烧火做饭、拉锯刨木，什么活都能干。人们看了觉得很神奇，于是一传十，十传百，最后传到了张金耳朵里。张金想：如果我把这绝活学到手，就能发大财了。于是，他就带上礼物来找师父。一进门，木头人就过来给他端茶倒水。他急忙跪下给王木匠磕头认错，并求师父教给他做木头人的绝活。王木匠淡淡地说:"你量一量这个木头人的尺寸,照样做一个就行了。"张金就把木头人拿起来,仔细量了一番,然后就动手做。可是做好后,木头人却不能动,改了几次也不行。张金又请教师父。王木匠说:"你是照我说的方法量的尺寸吗?"张金说:"是的。"王木匠说:"好,我看着你量,再试试。"于是,张金又量了一遍。师父看后笑着说:"你错了,你什么都量了,就是没量心!"张金听后,非常羞愧,脸一下子就红了。

后来,"没量心"这个说法就流传开了,由于"量"和"良"同音,渐渐演变成了"没良心"这个俗语,人们用它形容忘恩负义的人。

Legend has it that there was a carpenter named Wang in the ancient times. He knew all the tricks of the trade and enjoyed a good reputation in his hometown. Many people came to him to have furniture made. A young man named Zhang Jin wanted to learn carpentry from Wang. One day, he went to see Wang and told the latter of his intention. Wang said okay but there was a condition. "I am over 60 and have no children," he said. "If I can no longer work as a carpenter in my old age, will you support me?" Zhang said without hesitation that he would. "So long as you will teach me your skill, I shall support you in your old age. I shall be your son." He kowtowed to Wang.

Zhang Jin moved in Wang's house. At first he worked diligently and listened to his teacher, to whom he paid much respect. The carpenter treated him like his own son. He taught the young man many special skills. Zhang Jin could do his work independently after six months of learning. Then Zhang Jin worked as a carpenter in his own right and believed he could now make a living himself. He left Wang on the pretext that he was going to see his own parents. Wang waited but Zhang did not come back. He heard from others that Zhang was doing work independently. He felt very sorry. "Fortunately I didn't teach him my most special skill."

Soon Wang felt ill. He made a wooden man to serve him. The wooden man could cook meals and saw wood. It did all sorts of chores for Wang. People thought this was marvelous and the news spread until it reached Zhang Jin. Zhang Jin thought that if he had learned this skill, he would be able to make a lot of money. He brought some gifts with him to see his master. When he entered the house the wooden man offered him a cup of tea. He kowtowed to his master and acknowledged his mistake. He begged his master to teach him how to make a wooden man. "You can measure this wooden man and make a copy of it." His master said coolly. Zhang Jin measured the size of the wooden man and made a copy. But the wooden man he made couldn't move. He made several alterations, but couldn't make his wooden man work. Zhang Jin approached his master again. "Did you measure it according to the way I told you?" Zhang replied: "Yes." Wang said: "Let me see how did you measure it." Zhang Jin measured the wooden man again. "You had an error. You have measured everything except one. It's the heart." Zhang Jin heard the remark of his teacher and turned red in the face. He felt ashamed of himself.

Since then, this story has been repeatedly told by the Chinese people. As the words "measure heart" are homonymous with "conscience" in Chinese, thus the expression *mei liang xin* (haven't measured the heart) has come to mean being without conscience (heartless or being ungrateful).

千　金　小　姐

qiān　jīn　xiǎo　jiě

A GIRL WHO IS WORTH
ONE THOUSAND OUNCES OF GOLD

春秋时期，楚国的大将伍子胥的父亲—楚国大夫伍奢因直言而被楚平王所杀。伍子胥为避株连，连夜出逃，直奔楚国东部边境要地—昭关。当他逃出昭关，天已经快亮了。此时，他又饥又渴。没走多远，一条滔滔大江挡住了他的去路。伍子胥在江边俯下身子喝水，看见江水中自己的影子，不禁大吃一惊：只一夜工夫，两鬓已经斑白了。喝完水，伍子胥环顾四周，见江边有一户人家。他快步走进屋里，看见一位渔家姑娘在编织鱼网。姑娘一眼认出来人是大名鼎鼎的伍将军，急忙端来饭菜招待客人。伍子胥狼吞虎咽地匆匆吃完就告辞了。临走，他对姑娘说："若有追兵到来，千万不要说我伍子胥逃出了昭关。"姑娘说："请伍将军放心！"伍子胥往前走了几步，忽然又转身回来，对姑娘说："若有追兵到来，千万不要说我在你家吃过饭，否则会连累你家。"姑娘说："伍将军放心，请快过江去。"伍子胥走了几步，又转回身对姑娘说："你最好离开这里，以免被追兵盘问，受到纠缠。"姑娘见伍子胥这么担心，怕他再嘱咐下去，耽误了时间而被追兵赶上，急中生智，对伍子胥说："追兵来了！"伍子胥回头一看，不料姑娘"扑通"一声跳入江中。大江洪流滚滚，顷刻间姑娘就无影无踪了。伍子胥无法相救，便对着江面深深鞠了一躬，流着泪说道："姑娘，你为我献出了生命，我如果大难不死，战胜楚国，一定用一千两黄金为你建造庙宇，塑造金像。

追兵最终没能追上伍子胥，他取道宋国、郑国到了吴国，帮助吴王整顿军队，使吴国日益强盛。不久，吴国便攻破了楚国，伍子胥成了有功之臣。他把发生在江边的一段往事禀告了吴王。吴王拨给他一千两黄金，在江边建造了一座金碧辉煌的庙宇，并在庙中塑造了一尊渔家姑娘的金像。

此后，来过这庙里的人都说姑娘的品行高尚，贵值千金。"千金小姐"这个俗语便是从这个故事得来的。用作对大户人家年轻姑娘的尊称。

In the Spring and Autumn Period (770-476), Wu She, a senior official of the State of Chu and the father of a great general Wu Zixu, was killed for airing his views to Ping Wang, the King of Chu. To avoid becoming implicated in his father's crime, Wu Zixu fled at night from his home and sneaked out of Zhao Pass, a strategic gateway in the northeast border region. It was before dawn. Being hungry and thirsty, he came to a river. When he was drinking water from the river, he was shocked to see the reflection of himself in the water. His hair had turned gray overnight because of his worries. After he drank the water, he spotted a house. He walked quickly into the house where he saw a young girl weaving a fishnet. The girl at once recognized the famous general Wu Zixu. She gave him a meal. Wu devoured the food. Before he left the house, he said to the girl: "Don't tell the approaching army that I had escaped from Zhao Pass." The girl nodded. After taking a few steps, he turned back and said again: "Don't tell the army I had eaten a meal in your house." "Be rest assured, I won't," said the girl. "Please cross the river quickly." But after a while Wu Zixu again returned back to say: "You'd better leave here. Otherwise the army will ask you questions and you will be harassed by the soldiers." The girl saw that the general feared for her safety, which would cause delay in his escape. In her desperation she hit upon an idea and said: "The army has come. Go!" So saying she jumped into the river and disappeared from view. Wu Zixu was unable to save her life. He bowed to the river. Shedding tears, he said that if he succeeded in escaping from his predicament, he would spend one thousand ounces of gold to build a temple for the girl.

The pursuing army failed to capture Wu Zixu, who went to the State of Wu via the states of Song and Zheng. Wu Zixu helped the King of Wu to train his army. As a result, the State of Wu grew in strength. Not long after the State of Wu stormed the

State of Chu, Wu Zixu won great fame. He told the King of Wu what had happened to him when he was crossing the river during his flight. The king gave him one thousand ounces of gold to build a temple in memory of the fishing girl who had saved his life.

People who came to the temple to worship the statue of the girl all admired her integrity which matched the temple built with one thousand ounces of gold. This story thus gave rise to the expression "a girl who is worth one thousand ounces of gold." Today it is used as a term of respect for daughters from a great family.

一 言 出 口　泼 水 难 收

yì　yán　chū　kǒu　　pō　shuǐ　nán　shōu

A WORD SPOKEN CAN NEVER
BE TAKEN BACK AS SPILLED WATER
CAN NEVER BE GATHERED UP

西汉时，吴地有个穷书生，名叫朱买臣。他每天清早带上干粮上山砍柴，然后担上柴进城去卖。

由于朱买臣一心读书，不懂生意经，做买卖总是吃亏。因此，他的妻子和母亲便经常跟他一起上街卖柴。

就这样过了十多年，朱买臣一家的生活还是很穷苦。他的妻子想：这种苦日子，什么时候才能到头？每天背着柴沿街叫卖，太丢脸了！渐渐地，她开始嫌朱买臣无能，想离开他，只是一直没有机会说出口。

一天，朱买臣和妻子、母亲在官府门外卖柴，见一位老爷坐着轿子从里面出来，前呼后拥，威风凛凛。朱买臣的妻子感叹不已：为什么人与人竟会有这么大的差别呢！于是，她便向朱买臣提出要休夫，毅然决然地离开了他。不久，朱买臣的老母亲又因病去世了。

妻子离去，母亲去世，只剩下朱买臣孤身一人。他仍然一边砍柴谋生，一边读书，这样年复一年，又过了十几年。

朱买臣刻苦读书，学得满腹经纶，后来被任命为会稽（今浙江绍兴）太守。一天，他到民间察访，回到故乡，刚好遇到前妻。前妻见朱买臣做了官，非常后悔当初的决定，于是跪在马前，要求复合。朱买臣让随员取来一盆水，泼在地上，要前妻把水从地面上收起来。这怎么能办得到呢？朱买臣说"一言出口，泼水难收。我们之间的情义已尽，不可能再恢复从前的关系了！"前妻羞愧地退走了。

后来，"一言出口，泼水难收"这句俗语就流传开了。人们用它形容有些决定一旦作出，要想悔改是不可能的。

There was a poor scholar in the State of Wu during the Western Han Dynasty (206 B.C.-24 A.D.). His name was Zhu Maichen. He used to chop wood in the mountain every morning and sell the firewood in the city in the afternoon to eke out a living. As he was wholly devoted to study and ignorant in business, he usually made very little money from selling his firewood. His wife and mother had to go along with him so as to make more money.

The family lived this way for more than a decade and was still poor. His wife thought there was no way to escape from such a wretched life and felt shameful peddling firewood in the street everyday. She wanted a divorce but didn't find an opportunity to speak out her mind.

One day while Zhu Maichen and his wife were selling firewood in front of the residence of an official, they saw the official come out in a sedan chair, followed by his retinue in a dignified and awe-inspiring manner. Zhu's wife sighed, thinking that they and the official were all human beings. Why should such great difference exist between people? So she decided to ask and finally got a divorce with her husband. Soon after that Zhu Maichen's mother died of sickness.

With his marriage broken and mother dead, Zhu Maichen continued his studies as before, while still chopping wood for a living. Another decade passed. As a result of his diligent study he became a very learned man. Then he passed the imperial examination and was appointed Prefect of Kuaiji (now Shaoxing city, Zhejiang Province). One day, on an inspection tour to his hometown, he met his former wife. Seeing that her former husband had become an official, the woman went on her knees to beg that they be reunited. Zhu Maichen asked his attendant to take a basin of water and poured it on the ground. He told his former wife to collect the water from the ground. That was, of course, impossible. Zhu Maichen said: "Water once poured on the ground can never be collected. The same is true with words. Words once spoken can never be taken back!"

Hence the saying "a word spoken can never be taken back as spilled water can never be gathered up." Nowadays people use it to indicate that some decisions once made are forever irrevocable.

解 铃 还 需 系 铃 人

jiě líng hái xū xì líng rén

TO UNTIE THE BELL, THE MAN
WHO TIED IT IS REQUIRED

据说，有一次沙陀国（今河北宣化）的国王李克用上山打猎时，看见一只脖颈上系着一串响铃的斑斓猛虎，老虎每走一步，那串响铃便晃动一下，发出丁丁当当的声音，清脆悦耳。李克用觉得很有趣，便对随从的将士说："谁能解下虎颈上那串响铃，赏千两金，封万户侯！"重赏之下，必有勇夫。李克用话刚出口，就有十几员猛将跃下马背向那只猛虎扑去。结果，响铃没解下来，反而搭上了几员大将的性命。李克用见状大怒，翻身下马，打算亲自去跟那只猛虎搏斗。这时，有个谋士上前拦住他说："大王您不能去，治国的大业全靠您啊！"他又说："既然有人能把响铃系到猛虎脖颈上，此地一定有能降服猛虎的勇士，大王为什么不去寻访那个人呢？"当时沙陀国刚刚建立，正需要网罗各类人才，李克用点点头说："好！这件事就交给你去办吧！"谋士立即辞别李克用，带人去寻访那个能降服猛虎的人了。

　　三天后，那个谋士把一个小孩带到了李克用的王府。李克用见那小孩一脸稚气，只有十几岁的模样，半信半疑地问："虎颈上的那串响铃是你系上去的吗？""是我系的！"小孩把手里的一串响铃丢到李克用的面前，又说："你看，我又把它解下来了！"李克用见到响铃，又惊又喜，便将那小孩收为养子，赐名李存勖。这李存勖长大后成了威震天下的打虎英雄。

　　后来，人们从这个故事中引申出"解铃还需系铃人"这句俗语，用来说明是谁惹出的事，还必须让谁去解决。

Legend has it that Li Keyong, king of the State of Shatuo (now Xuanhua, Hebei Province) went to the mountains on a hunting expedition. He saw a tiger with a bell on its neck. As the tiger stalked in the mountain, the bell rang in clear and pleasant notes. Li Keyong was quite intrigued by it. He said to the accompanying generals that he would reward anyone with one thousand ounces of gold and the title of marquis if he could untie the bell from the tiger's neck. A few generals jumped to the back of the tiger and tried to untie the bell. But they all lost their lives in the attempt. Li Keyong was in a rage and got off from his horse, deciding to fight against the tiger himself. One of his strategists stopped him, saying: "You must not go. The kingdom has to be ruled by a king. Since there is a man who had tied the bell on the tiger neck there in the first place, there must be a man who can untie it. Why not find this man? At that time, the State of Shatuo had just been established, the kingdom was in need of many talented men. Li agreed to the suggestion and told the strategist to find the man. The strategist bade good-bye to the king and went out with his subordinates to find the man. Three days later the strategist brought back with him a lad to the princely establishment of Li Keyong. Seeing the lad was so young, Li only half-believed that he had put the bell on the neck of the tiger. The lad said: "Yes, I did that." As he answered, he threw the bell in front of King Li, who was surprised but happy. Li asked the lad whether he was willing to be with the king or not. Then the king made the boy his adopted son and gave him the name Li Cunxun. The lad grew up with a great reputation as a legendary tiger-tamer.

The saying, "To untie the bell, the man who tied it is required," was derived from the aforementioned story. Today people use it to mean that whoever started the trouble should end it.

秀才不出门， 便知天下事

xiù cái bù chū mén   biàn zhī tiān xià shì

WITHOUT GOING OUTDOORS, A SCHOLAR KNOWS ALL THE WORLD'S AFFAIRS

古时候，一户人家有兄弟两人。老大是个秀才，念了很多书，天文地理无所不知，古今中外无事不晓。而弟弟却不识字。由于哥哥博学多才，村里的人遇到难办的事都来找他，并给他一个美称叫"万事通"。可弟弟却不服气，心想，一定要找一件哥哥不知道的事来为难他，让人们也来请教我。

第二天，天还没亮，弟弟就不辞而别。

他边走边寻，下决心要找到天下最奇怪的东西。一天他来到一座大森林边，只见茫茫暮色，莽莽密林。他爬上高高的山石，发现不远处有两点光亮，忙拔脚奔去。到了跟前，那光却熄灭了，哪里有什么人家，原来是一棵两人也抱不拢的老树。他捡起一块石头，往树上掷去，只听"啪"的一声，那两盏灯又亮了。他定神一看，原来是一只大鸟的眼睛。那鸟受了惊吓，展开翅膀飞走了。

弟弟在密林里越走越深，暗暗叫苦。忽然听到了狗叫的声音，心想：有狗的地方，前面一定有人家。当他循声走近时，看见一棵比刚才那棵树还要大得多的古树。就在这时，那声音又从头顶上传来。他想爬上树去看看，无奈天黑，只好等天亮再说。好不容易熬到天亮，发现那怪声是从树顶上一对大鸟嘴里发出来的。他爬上树想看个究竟，发现树顶上有一个鸟窝，窝里铺的是灵芝草，草底下排着三个四四方方的蛋。此时弟弟又惊又喜，想：这件奇事一定能难住哥哥。

弟弟连忙往回赶，一到家里，就拿出带回的鸟蛋问哥哥。哥哥接过蛋看了看，便拿来文房四宝，写下一首诗："金翅大鹏鸟，窝是灵芝草，生的四方蛋，啼声像狗叫，两眼似灯笼，双翅光闪耀，常住森林里，古树好为巢。"

弟弟见哥哥说的一点也不差，就问："你没出屋半步，怎么知道得这么清楚。"哥说："多读书就能知天下事。"弟弟这才心服口服，也懂得了读书的好处。从此，他逢人就讲："秀才不出门，便知天下事。我们不读书，什么也不懂，就算懂了，也要多跑几百里路哩。"

于是，"秀才不出门，便知天下事"这句话就传开了。久而久之，就成了一句俗语。人们用它说明一个人如果博览群书，知识面就会很广。

A long time ago, there were two brothers who lived together in the same house. The elder brother was a *xiucai*, i.e., a scholar who had passed the imperial examination at the county level. Having read many books, he had a wide range of knowledge. Many people came to him for consultation to solve problems. He earned the nickname: know-it-all. His younger brother was illiterate but refuse to acknowledge the ability of his elder brother. He said to himself: I'll ask my brother something that he doesn't know so as to prove I know better than him, so that people will come to me for consultation.

The younger brother left the house the next day.

He came to a forest. It was already dark when he came to the depth of the forest. When he climbed to the top of a high rock, he saw not far away two gleams of light. He thought there might be a household there. He hurriedly went over but couldn't find any house there. He found a tree so big that two men could not enclose its circumference with extended arms. He picked up a stone and threw it at the tree top. The stone fell to the ground with a thud. The two lights shone again. It turned out to be the two eyes of a big bird who got frightened and flew away.

The younger brother walked on and penetrated further into the depth of the forest. He felt uneasy. Suddenly he heard the sound of barking. He was delighted. If there was a dog, there would be some inhabitants around. As he walked in the direction of the dog bark, he saw an ancient tree of even bigger size. The sound came from the top of the tree. He wanted to climb to the tree top but it was dark. He had to wait till dawn. He discovered that the sound came from two big birds. He climbed to the top of the tree and found a bird nest. The nest was built with *lingzhi*, a kind of magic fungus. Beneath the *lingzhi* were three square-shaped eggs. The younger brother was surprised but happy. He said to himself: this is a strange encounter. It will certainly baffle my elder brother.

Immidiately after the younger brother had got home, he produced the bird eggs in front of the elder brother. The elder brother took out his stationery and wrote: "A roc with golden wings/ Its nest is built with *lingzhi*/ It lays square eggs/ And barks like a dog/ Eyes are like lanterns/ Wings are shimmering in the night/ Its habitat is in the forest/ A nest built on a tree." The younger brother saw that his elder brother said everything right. He asked: "You didn't leave the house. How is it that you know everything so well?" The elder brother replied: "I read many books. So I know many things about the world." Finally the younger brother acknowledged his brother's ability and realized the benefit of reading. He told people, "Without going outdoors, a scholar knows all the world's affairs. We know nothing because we don't read. Even if we get to know something, it will cost us a journey of several hundred *li* on foot to find out."

This story thus gave rise to the saying. Today it is used to describe a well-read person who can acquire a broad range of knowledge just through books.

"横七竖八" 和 "乱七八糟"

héng qī shù bā　　　hé　　luàn qī bā zāo

SEVEN ON A HORIZONTAL LINE
AND EIGHT VERTICALLY
AND SEVEN HERE EIGHT THERE

从前，每年夏至这一天，清朝宫廷里都要举行一次种稻仪式。乾隆皇帝要亲自到宫殿外面的一块空地上，站在正中央，文武大臣分列两边。站在高处的大太监先喊四句："国以民为本，民以食为天。万岁来种地，廪仓处处填。"大太监喊声刚落，小太监就捧出一个金盘，跑着，呈递给乾隆。这金盘上有七颗金黄的稻种。乾隆抓起稻种往地上一撒，就算种过了。然后在一片欢呼声中回宫去了。

有一年，乾隆下江南巡察，到了苏州。这时正是黄梅季节，家家户户忙着栽秧。乾隆想看看江南农夫栽秧的情景，便换了一身商人服饰，带了一个扮作仆人的小太监，来到田边。

过去栽秧有个规矩，要看第一个人。这个人在最前面，先用绳子在田里圈出栽秧的范围，然后，站在田边的农夫把扎好的一把把秧苗往秧田里栽，规定是横着栽七棵，竖着栽八棵，这叫"横七竖八"。一把秧苗恰好栽一行，栽得不好，秧苗不是根朝上，就是歪倒在田里。

乾隆看了一会儿，觉得乡下栽秧和他在宫里"种稻"不一样，很是有趣。就学着种田人的样子，下田栽秧去了。他手里拿了一把秧苗，还没有栽几行，秧苗就都用光了。再一看田里，秧苗有的根朝上，有的歪倒了，不是"横七竖八"，倒是"乱七八糟"了。

据说"横七竖八"和"乱七八糟"的俗语就是从这里来的。

On summer solstice every year, a ceremony was held by the royal court in the Qing Dynasty (1644-1911) in Beijing, in which Emperor Qianlong personally planted rice seeds to mark the planting season. The ceremony took place in an empty spot in front of the palace. The emperor stood in the center, flanked by two rows of officials on each side. A top eunuch official announced, "The masses of people were the foundation of the state, to whom food was of vital importance. As His Majesty had personally come to till the land, the granaries would be filled everywhere." The eunuch would take out a golden plate containing seven rice seeds and presented them to the emperor, who would throw the seeds onto the ground. This was supposed to be the cultivation of the land by the monarch. Following this formality, the emperor would return to his palace amidst thunderous applause.

Legend has it that during one of his imperial inspection tours in south China, Qianlong arrived in Suzhou. It was in the rainy season. Every household was busily selecting seeds prior to planting. Qianlong wanted to see how farmers in south China planted seeds. He dressed himself as a merchant, accompanied by a young eunuch as attendant and walked to the paddy field.

Planting was done in the old days according to specific rules. The first man led the way. He measured the size of the plot with a rope for planting. The bundles of seedlings would be thrown into the field. Seedlings were planted according to the following patterns: seven on a horizontal line and eight vertically. One bundle of seedlings were planted in a row. If planting was not done properly, the seedlings would be upside down or tilt to one side.

Qianlong found that the way he planted in the court was quite different from the way the people actually did. He was rather intrigued by this. He followed the example of the farmer and went into the paddy field to sow seedlings. Pretty soon he used up all the seedlings. He saw what he had done was not in accordance with the pattern "seven on a horizontal line and eight vertically," but rather "seven here eight there."

This story of how the emperor planted seedlings gave rise to the saying "seven on a horizontal line and eight vertically and seven here eight there." It is synonymous with the English expression "at sixes and sevens" which means in utter disarray, a total mess.

墙 上 挂 竹 帘 ── 没 门

qiáng shang guà zhú lián   méi mén

HANGING A BAMBOO CURTAIN
ON THE WALL ─ NO DOOR
IN FRONT OF YOU

从前，上党有个有名的画匠名叫张才，擅长画荷花。方圆百里的人都夸他画的荷花活灵活现，像刚刚从枝上折下来一样。张才听到人们奉承他，便自命不凡起来，很是高傲，扬言天下无对手。另有一个秀才李真，不仅通晓诗书，且精于绘画。一天，李真进京赶考，路过上党，听说张才很会画荷花，便想与他结交。不料张才自恃才高。竟不接见。这下惹恼了李真，要与张才比个高低。

　　一天，天刚亮，李真便在集市上占了个清静的地方，在白壁上作了一幅画，只等张才到来。张才吃过早饭来到集市上，见一秀才已在那里，也不打招呼，铺开画幅等游人来买。不久，街上人如潮涌，买画的人不计其数，一会儿就卖完了。李真见张才画已卖完，上前问道："先生的画着实画得活灵活现，不知尊姓大名？"张才见其早早来到，却没有卖出几张画，便问："你是什么人，敢来问我？难道连我张才的大名也不知？"李真并不在意，答道："小生李真，初到此地，多有冒犯，家中备有薄酒一杯，为先生赔礼。请进！"张才抬头一看，见一竹帘挂在门上，也不还礼，想要进去。可是双手几次掀那竹帘也掀不起，正在疑虑，李秀才又说：请先生仔细辨别，切莫动手。"当时，张秀才与众人细细辨认，原来并无竹帘子，而是一幅画。

　　这时，人人拍手称奇，张才羞愧不已。人们由这个故事引申出俗语"墙上挂竹帘一没门"，形容某事决不可能办到，后来多用作拒绝别人时说的话。

There was a well-known painter called Zhang Cai who lived in Shangdang (in present Shanxi Province). Good at painting lotuses, he was praised for his vivid depiction of the flower by people in neighboring counties. It was said that the lotus he painted was so realistic that it looked as if it had just been plucked from the pond. Zhang Cai became rather conceited. He openly declared that he had no equal when it came to painting lotuses. There was a *xiucai* called Li Zhen, who not only was well read in classics and poetry but excelled in painting as well. One day, Li Zhen took a trip to the capital to take part in an imperial examination. When he arrived in Shangdang, he heard about Zhang Cai and was anxious to make the acquaintance of the man. As Zhang Cai was a conceited person, when Li called, Zhang would not even see him. This annoyed Li Zhen. He decided to compete with Zhang Cai in painting.

At the break of day, Li Zhen sat in a quiet corner in the marketplace. He painted a picture on the wall and waited. Zhang Cai finished his breakfast and came to the market. He saw a *xiucai* was already there. Without greeting the *xiucai*, Zhang Cai took out his paintings, waiting for buyers. The people poured into the marketplace. There were many buyers among them. Seeing Zhang Cai had sold all his paintings, Li Zhen went to Zhang Cai and complimented him on his graphic and vivid paintings. "May I have your name?" asked Li Zhen. Zhang Cai saw that Li Zhen had come early to the market but sold only a few paintings. He said proudly, "Who are you? How dare you ask me such questions? Don't you know that my name is Zhang Cai?" Li Zhen didn't seem to be bothered by Zhang Cai's remark. He replied: "My name is Li Zhen. I am here for the first time. Perhaps I have offended you. I have some wine in my place. Please come over. I wish to apologize to you for being impolite to you." Zhang Cai lifted up his head and saw a bamboo curtain hanging on the door. He wanted to go into the house and tried to lift up the curtain. He did this several times but couldn't. He began to have doubts. "Please look at the curtain carefully. Don't try to lift it though," said Li. Zhang Cai now looked carefully at the bamboo curtain, together with all the others. He discovered to his dismay that that was not a curtain — but a painting. People were amazed and clapped their hands in admiration. Zhang Cai felt ashamed of himself for his ignorance.

The expression, "Hanging a bamboo curtain on the wall — no door in front of you," evolved from this story. It describes something that simply cannot be done. It also means that you turn down a request by somebody who asks you for a favor.

（京）新登字 136 号

图书在版编目（CIP）数据

轻松学俗语：中英对照/申俊，马汉民编．
－北京：新世界出版社，1998.2
ISBN 7 - 80005 - 373 - 3

I.轻··· II.①申···②马···
III.①对外汉语教学－语言读物②汉语－俗语－汉、英
IV.H195.5

策　　划：姜汉忠
责任编辑：宋　鹤
版面设计：朱桉青

轻 松 学 俗 语

申 俊　马汉民　编

*

新世界出版社出版

（北京百万庄路 24 号）

邮政编码 100037

北京外文印刷厂印刷

中国国际图书贸易总公司发行

（中国北京车公庄西路 35 号）

北京邮政信箱第 399 号　邮政编码 100044

新华书店北京发行所国内发行

1998 年（汉英）第一版　1998 年北京第一次印刷

850 × 1168 毫米 1/32 开本

ISBN 7 - 80005 - 373 - 3/G · 088

02200

9 - CE - 3247P